OCCASIONAL PAPER 209

Methodology for Current Account and Exchange Rate Assessments

Peter Isard, Hamid Faruqee, G. Russell Kincaid,
and Martin Fetherston

INTERNATIONAL MONETARY FUND
Washington DC
2001

Production: IMF Graphics Section
Figures: Sanaa Elaroussi
Typesetting: Alicia Etchebarne-Bourdin

Cataloging-in-Publication Data

Methodology for current account and exchange rate assessments/Peter Isard . . . [et al.]—Washington, D.C.: International Monetary Fund, 2001.

p. cm.—(Occasional paper, 0251-6365); 209

Includes bibliographical references

ISBN 1-58906-081-4

1. Foreign exchange rates. 2. Balance of payments. 3. International Monetary Fund. I. Isard, Peter. II. International Monetary Fund. III. Occasional paper (International Monetary Fund); no. 209

HG3821.M35 2001

Price: US$20.00
(US$17.50 to full-time faculty members and
students at universities and colleges)

Please send orders to:
International Monetary Fund, Publication Services
700 19th Street, N.W., Washington, D.C. 20431, U.S.A.
Tel.: (202) 623-7430 Telefax: (202) 623-7201
E-mail: publications@imf.org
Internet: http://www.imf.org

recycled paper

Contents

The following symbols have been used throughout this paper:

. . . to indicate that data are not available;

— to indicate that the figure is zero or less than half the final digit shown, or that the item does not exist;

– between years or months (e.g., 2000–01 or January–June) to indicate the years or months covered, including the beginning and ending years or months;

/ between years (e.g., 2000/01) to indicate a fiscal (financial) year.

"Billion" means a thousand million.

Minor discrepancies between constituent figures and totals are due to rounding.

The term "country," as used in this paper, does not in all cases refer to a territorial entity that is a state as understood by international law and practice; the term also covers some territorial entities that are not states, but for which statistical data are maintained and provided internationally on a separate and independent basis.

Preface

In carrying out its bilateral and multilateral surveillance responsibilities, the IMF needs to make judgments about the consistency between prevailing exchange rates and medium-run fundamentals. This paper discusses the methodologies used by the IMF staff, pointing to conceptual and empirical limitations and to various issues that arise in interpreting the assessments. These methodologies will continue to evolve over time in response to efforts to strengthen the existing framework.

Among the IMF staff, much of the responsibility for shaping consensus on methodology and conducting exchange rate assessments has been assigned to the interdepartmental Coordinating Group on Exchange Rate Issues (CGER). CGER was established in 1995 under the cochairmanship of representatives from the Policy Development and Review Department and the Research Department, and with active participation of the IMF's area departments. The authors of this paper have each played a major role in CGER's work. Russell Kincaid held the Policy Development and Review Department cochair position from fall 1998 to spring 2001, Martin Fetherston is currently the Policy Development and Review Department cochair, Peter Isard has been cochair for the Research Department, and Hamid Faruqee has made central contributions to the methodological framework while also facilitating the assessment exercises in numerous ways. The general direction of CGER's analytical work has been guided mainly by Stanley Fischer, the First Deputy Managing Director of the IMF (through August 2001), Michael Mussa, the Economic Counsellor and Director of the Research Department (through July 2001), and Jack Boorman, Counsellor and Director of the Policy Development and Review Department (through November 2001).

The paper has benefited from discussion at an IMF Executive Board seminar in June 2001. The authors are also grateful for numerous comments and suggestions received from Thomas Krueger and other colleagues on the IMF staff, to Susanna Mursula and Sarma Jayanthi for research assistance, and to Victoria Ashiru and Dawn Heaney for preparing the manuscript. Esha Ray of the External Relations Department edited the manuscript and coordinated production of the publication.

I Overview

Surveillance over the exchange rate policies of its member countries is a central responsibility of the International Monetary Fund. In late 1994, the IMF staff took a step toward making its surveillance more effective by initiating more extensive and systematic assessments of the current account positions and exchange rates of the major industrial countries, incorporating both the perspectives of the IMF's area departments and calculations derived from a multilateral framework implemented by the IMF Research Department. In 1995, an interdepartmental working group, the Coordinating Group on Exchange Rate Issues (CGER), was established to strengthen and extend this work, and to provide a greater degree of discipline and consistency in the staff's judgments about exchange rates. CGER's general approach for assessing the current accounts and exchange rates of the major industrial countries was reviewed by the IMF's Executive Board in October 1997, and a description of the methodology was subsequently made public.[1]

This paper reports further on CGER's work, as reviewed by the IMF's Executive Board in June 2001. It provides perspectives on alternative frameworks for assessing exchange rates and the rationale for CGER's general approach (Section II and Appendix I); it updates the description of the methodology for assessing the current accounts and exchange rates of industrial countries, pointing to the relative strengths and weaknesses of CGER's analytic framework and the judgments involved in deriving and interpreting the quantitative assessments (Section II and Appendixes II and III); it describes some initial efforts to develop a separate methodology for assessing the current account positions of emerging market economies (Section III and Appendix IV); and it concludes with a brief summary (Section IV). The focus of this paper is on methodology and interpretive issues, rather than on numerical assessments.

CGER's work on industrial countries is motivated by the wide fluctuations that have occurred in exchange rates among major currencies during recent decades. As illustrated by Figure 1, both the nominal and real effective (weighted-average) exchange rates of major currencies have frequently exhibited prolonged movements in one direction followed by pronounced reversals. One case in point is the dramatic rise of the U.S. dollar during the first half of the 1980s, followed by an equally large drop between early 1985 and early 1987. The Japanese yen and the pound sterling have also been pushed to sharply appreciated and depreciated levels a number of times over the past two decades, and similar wide variation is evident for weighted-average exchange rates of the deutsche mark against the currencies of countries outside the euro area.

Economists have achieved reasonable success in developing an understanding of the relationships between exchange rates and macroeconomic fundamentals over the *medium run* and, hence, of the trends in exchange rates over time. In particular, trends in nominal exchange rates tend to reflect inflation differentials over the medium run, and real exchange rates tend to gravitate toward levels at which the associated current account imbalances are fairly moderate in size and consistent with factors that influence the relative saving and investment positions of different countries over the medium run. It has also been demonstrated formally that the *short-run* behavior of exchange rates includes a large unpredictable component. Although a consensus has emerged on partial explanations for some of the large deviations of currency values from their medium-run trends, such as the impact of the shift in the U.S. policy mix in pushing the dollar higher in 1980–82, for the most part changes in macroeconomic fundamentals have not provided convincing and generally accepted explanations for the wide swings in exchange rates. This has contributed to the view that market exchange rates sometimes become substantially misaligned with medium-run macroeconomic fundamentals.

Wide swings in real exchange rates have major effects on countries' competitiveness, which can have significant implications for the growth and composition of economic activity and employ-

[1] Isard and Faruqee (1998).

Figure 1. Selected Industrial Countries: Nominal and Real Effective Exchange Rates, January 1980–January 2001[1]
(1990=100; logarithmic scale)

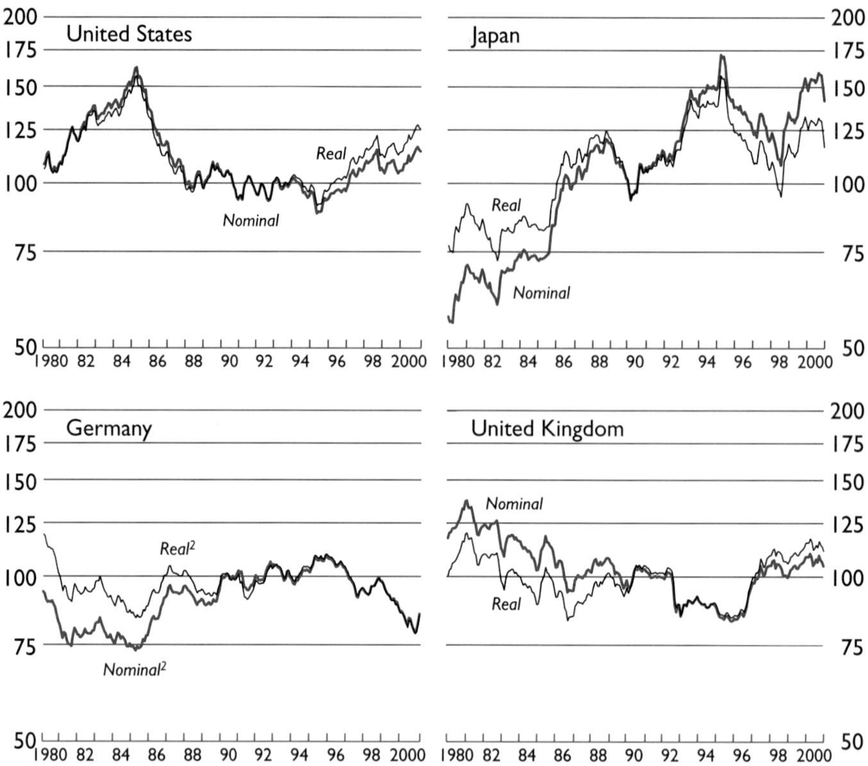

Source: IMF, *International Financial Statistics.*
[1]Real effective exchange rates are based on consumer price indices. Increases correspond to appreciations.
[2]Weighted averages against trading partners outside the euro area.

ment.[2] Moreover, the potential for substantial nominal and real effects of large exchange rate changes complicates the task of monetary policy, sometimes adding significantly to the difficulties of keeping economies expanding at close to full potential and with low inflation. Accordingly, the behavior of exchange rates is a relevant concern for policymakers. In making policy decisions, it can be important to assess by how much prevailing exchange rates deviate from the levels that are consistent with medium-run fundamentals—or, equivalently, the levels toward which exchange rates seem likely to gravitate over time.

In providing guidance to IMF staff, the Executive Board has stressed that the IMF's views on possible misalignments should be communicated in a timely and confidential manner to the authorities concerned. In light of the considerable difficulties in estimating equilibrium exchange rates, the IMF has generally not taken a public posture on exchange rate misalignments. On a number of occasions, however, CGER's assessments have provided a basis for the staff and management to express qualitative judgments about exchange rates among the major currencies, both in the context of the World Economic Outlook (WEO) and in meetings of the Group of Seven and other international fora. The assessments have also been employed by the IMF's area departments in their dialogues with national authorities during Article IV consultations with industrial countries, and in some cases the assessments for individual countries have appeared in published staff reports. CGER revisits its assessments semiannually in association with the updating of the WEO projections.

[2]In addition, sharp currency appreciations often give rise to political pressures to protect exchange-rate-sensitive sectors of the economy from foreign competition.

II A Methodology for Assessments of Industrial Countries

Background and Caveats

The quantification of equilibrium exchange rates is a somewhat murky area of economics. Conceptual frameworks typically rely on strong simplifying assumptions, and the empirical support for different approaches is mixed. From a policymaking perspective, however, such exercises are important: the IMF cannot effectively exercise its surveillance responsibilities without forming views about possible misalignments of exchange rates and considering the risks of sudden and sharp corrections of currency misalignments.

Success in explaining the behavior of exchange rates—and, hence, in providing meaningful empirical support for methodologies of assessing equilibrium exchange rates in terms of economic fundamentals—depends importantly on time horizons. Based largely on research that flourished during the 1970s and early 1980s, economists have concluded that models of the links between currency values and economic fundamentals perform little if any better than random walks in predicting the behavior of exchange rates in the short run.[3] Furthermore, from surveys of commercial banks and other private financial institutions that actively participate in exchange markets, policymakers have learned that market participants condition their short-run trading strategies to a large extent on "technical analysis" of very recent trends or other patterns in the observed behavior of exchange rates, although they regard fundamentals as much more important than technical analysis in their long-term decision making.[4] These perspectives discredit the notion that exchange rates should be expected to adjust, in the short run, to fundamentals-based equilibrium levels.[5]

[3]Meese and Rogoff (1983a, 1983b, 1988). Numerous attempts to overturn the Meese-Rogoff results have failed; see Rogoff (1999) and the survey by Frankel and Rose (1995). Moreover, as emphasized by Flood and Rose (1999), the short-run volatility of exchange rates far exceeds the volatility of macroeconomic fundamentals.

[4]Group of Ten Deputies (1993).

[5]Economists have also had limited success in finding fundamentals-based explanations for the short-run behavior of the prices of assets other than foreign exchange—for example, equity prices.

Partly for that reason, most methodologies for defining equilibrium exchange rates have relied on models of behavior over a medium- or long-run horizon.[6]

One traditional methodology for defining equilibrium exchange rates is the purchasing power parity (PPP) approach, which hypothesizes that the nominal exchange rate between any two currencies should reflect closely the relative purchasing powers of the two monetary units, as indicated by national price levels.[7] It is commonly expressed as a hypothesis that, over a given period of time, the percentage change in the nominal exchange rate between any two currencies will equal the difference between the percentage changes in the price levels of the two corresponding countries—or, equivalently, that the real exchange rate between the two currencies remains constant.

Although PPP has been discredited as a hypothesis about the relationship between exchange rates and national price levels in the short run,[8] the econometric evidence is much more favorable to PPP as a hypothesis about medium-run or long-run behavior.[9] This is illustrated by Figure 2. Changes in nominal exchange

[6]The dramatic changes that have occurred in the size of financial asset holdings, and in the amounts of these holdings that can be moved rapidly between countries and/or currencies, have led some to suggest that the short-run behavior of exchange rates can be explained in terms of capital flows and that current account flows have a relatively minor influence. This view can be misleading in two senses. First, although exchange rate movements and capital flows may be closely associated in the short run, it would be misleading to regard capital flows as more than a proximate cause of exchange rate movements; a deeper understanding of the short-run behavior of exchange rates would require an understanding of the factors that drive capital flows. Second, because the capital account and current account are linked by the balance of payments identity, it would be misleading to suggest that the behavior of exchange rates is more closely related to the capital account than to the current account.

[7]The term purchasing power parity was coined in the early twentieth century by Cassel (1918, 1922).

[8]Whether one looks at consumer price indices, GDP deflators, wholesale price indices, unit labor costs, or export price indices, there is considerable month-to-month and quarter-to-quarter variation in the associated measures of real exchange rates. Hyperinflations provide exceptional circumstances in which PPP has not been discredited as a description of short-run behavior.

[9]See Breuer (1994), Isard (1995), Froot and Rogoff (1995), and Rogoff (1996) for summary discussions.

Figure 2. Exchange Rate Changes Versus Inflation Differentials Over Different Time Intervals[1]

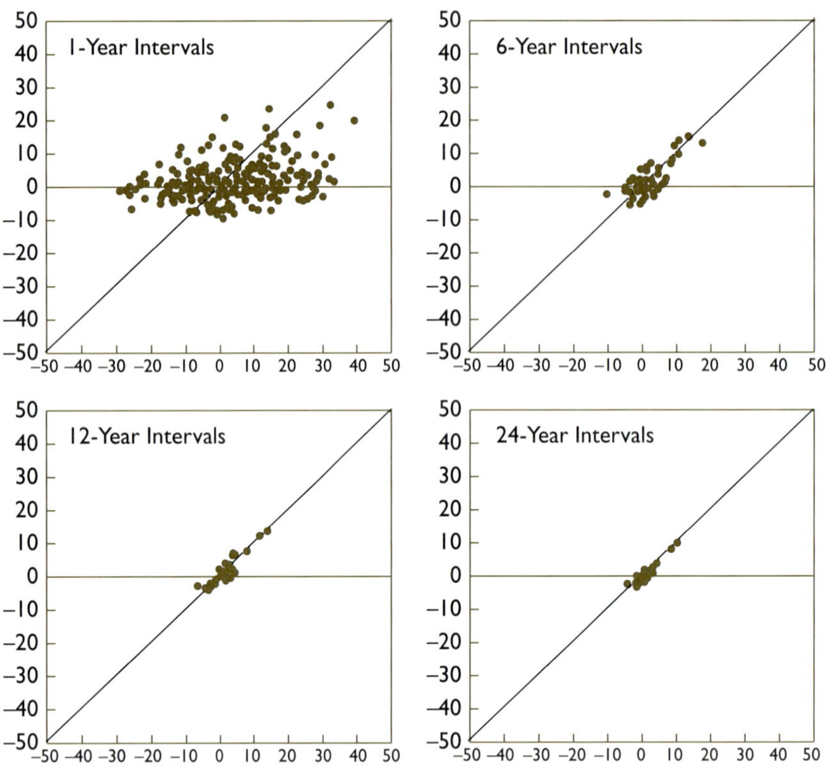

[1]Based on Flood and Taylor (1996). The plots are constructed from annual average data on the nominal exchange rates of 20 industrial country currencies versus the U.S. dollar, along with corresponding consumer price indices, for the period 1976–2000. Changes in exchange rates are measured along the horizontal axes; changes in CPIs along the vertical axes. The first panel plots 480 one-year changes (24 for each country); the second plots 80 nonoverlapping six-year changes (at annual rates) corresponding to the periods 1976–82, 1982–88, 1988–94, and 1994–2000; and so forth.

rates are measured along the horizontal axis, inflation differentials are measured along the vertical axis, and the diagonal 45 degree line represents the set of points that are consistent with the PPP hypothesis. The figure shows that PPP becomes a much more respectable hypothesis as the time horizon is lengthened, and that—at least over the past quarter century—the long-run PPP hypothesis fits the data for industrial countries remarkably well.[10]

Policymakers have relied on the PPP formula on various occasions to help them decide whether, and by how much, to adjust *nominal* exchange rates. Such use of the PPP formula to calculate an appropriate or "equilibrium" level for the nominal exchange rate requires a decision about the type of price (or cost) index on which the calculations are to be based, as well as an assumption about the equilibrium level of the *real* exchange rate. The latter is generally taken to be the observed level of the real exchange rate during some selected base year, or the average level of the real exchange rate over an extended period of time.

Sensitivity to the price (or cost) measure and base period that are chosen limits the usefulness of PPP as a normative approach. Figure 3 plots five measures of the real exchange rate between the pound sterling and the deutsche mark from 1970 through 2000. Each of the measures suggests that the pound was

[10]The fit is not as close for the developing countries or for the industrial countries over the previous quarter century. Indeed, as elaborated in the discussion of the Balassa-Samuelson hypothesis in Appendix I, there is empirical evidence of systematic deviations from PPP.

Figure 3. Real Exchange Rates Between the United Kingdom and Germany, 1970–2000
(1970=100)

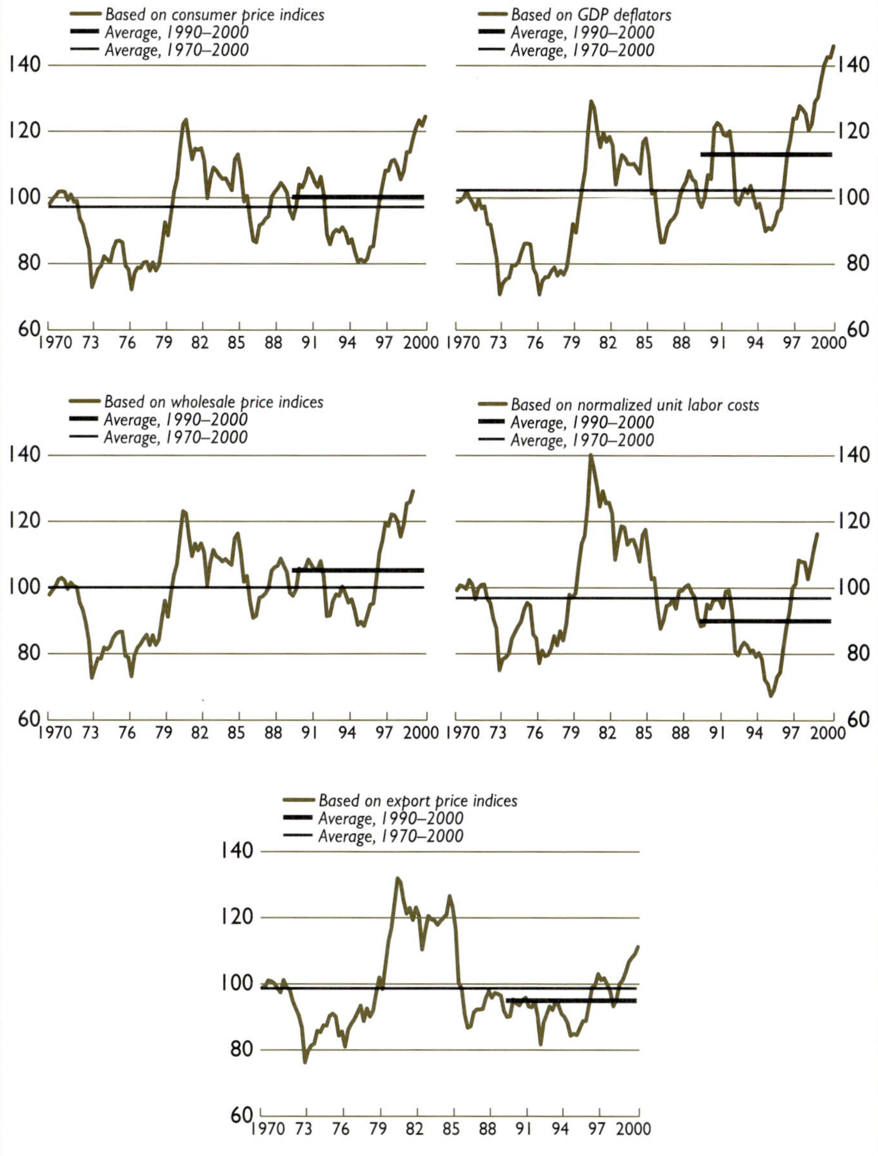

Sources: IMF, *International Financial Statistics*; and IMF staff calculations.

stronger than its equilibrium rate (proxied by long-term averages) against the deutsche mark (hence, the euro) in 2000; but the magnitude of the estimated deviation from equilibrium ranges from 10 percent to 40 percent, depending on the type of price or cost index used and the averaging period chosen.

Given the limitations of the PPP hypothesis as a normative approach, economists have been attracted to other methodologies for assessing exchange rates. CGER relies heavily on the macroeconomic balance approach, which makes quantitative assessments of exchange rates that are consistent with "appropriate" current account positions (external balance) when economies are operating at potential output (internal balance). Other approaches include an extended PPP methodology that takes account of Balassa-Samuelson effects, estimated reduced-form models of exchange rate behavior, and the approach of relying on general equilibrium frameworks. Appendix I outlines these alternative approaches and why CGER has chosen not to rely on them.

Key features of the macroeconomic balance approach have been prominent in calculations by the IMF staff since at least as far back as 1967, when views were developed about the appropriate size of the prospective devaluation of sterling.[11] As refined by the IMF staff during the 1970s and early 1980s,[12] and also used by Williamson (1985) and others in their early work on "fundamental equilibrium exchange rates" (FEERs), the macroeconomic balance approach was rooted in the balance of payments identity. In particular, these applications tended to define external balance in terms of "balanced" or "normal" or "target" or "underlying" capital flows, and then estimated the levels of real exchange rates that would equate current account balances—at positions of internal balance—to these notions of equilibrium capital flows. By contrast, CGER applications, as elaborated below, are rooted in the national income accounting identity that links the current account to the saving-investment balance. While the two identities are closely related, the shift in emphasis has been in the direction of relying less on ad hoc judgments about equilibrium capital flows, which are difficult to make in an environment of high and rising capital mobility, and more on models of the behavior of the saving-investment balance over the medium run.[13]

It is important to recognize at the outset that CGER's analysis is subject to considerable limitations in generating definitive estimates and to various caveats in interpreting the assessments. A key limitation is that the quantitative assessments are inherently imprecise. In general, economists do not have the conceptual basis or empirical methodology for generating precise estimates of the exchange rate levels that are consistent with medium-run macroeconomic fundamentals. As will become evident below, imprecision enters CGER's quantitative analysis in several different places. Such imprecision provides the rationale for generating assessments with both the macroeconomic balance framework and a PPP approach, and for characterizing CGER's summary assessments as approximations or ranges that involve a significant element of judgment.

A further important caveat is that large deviations of exchange rates from their medium-run equilibrium levels (even if these could be estimated precisely) do not necessarily represent currency misalignments. In some cases, such deviations may reflect short-term cyclical factors rather than medium-run disequilibria. Moreover, regardless of their cause, deviations of exchange rates from medium-run equilibrium can sometimes be helpful from a short-run perspective; in particular, an appreciated currency can help cool an overheated economy, just as a depreciated currency can help reinvigorate a weak one. Furthermore, quite apart from cyclical considerations, deviations of exchange rates from medium-run equilibrium sometimes reflect a need for policy adjustment rather than an indication that markets are wrong.

Two related points should be kept in mind when interpreting CGER's assessments. First, the assessment that a currency is substantially stronger or weaker than its medium-run equilibrium level does not necessarily imply a high probability of a sudden and sharp correction. Consequently, it is difficult to evaluate the assessments on the basis of their track record in anticipating exchange rate movements. The failure of the U.S. dollar to weaken significantly since early 1997, when CGER began to assess it as substantially stronger than its medium-run equilibrium level, can be interpreted as either a persistent error in CGER's analysis or an implication of the possibility that deviations from medium-run equilibrium can be persistent. Second, there is no general answer to the question of whether policy actions should be taken when exchange rates appear to deviate substantially from their medium-run equilibrium values. The latter issue needs to be addressed on a case-by-case basis in the context of a broader assessment of macroeconomic circumstances.

Macroeconomic Balance Assessments

As noted earlier, the macroeconomic balance framework is based on the accounting identity that links a country's current account balance *(CUR)* to the excess of domestic saving *(S)* over domestic investment *(I)*.[14]

[11]See Polak (1995), who emphasizes the focus on external balance and the use of elasticity calculations but does not mention internal balance. The macroeconomic balance approach apparently began to take shape in the writings of Nurkse (1945) and Metzler (1951) and benefited from pathbreaking contributions by Meade (1951) and Swan (1963).

[12]Artus (1978) and Artus and Knight (1984).

[13]See, for example, Knight and Masson (1988), Williamson (1994), Clark and others (1994), Debelle and Faruqee (1996), Isard and Faruqee (1998), and Faruqee, Isard, and Masson (1999).

[14]There are some definitional distinctions between national accounts concepts and balance of payments concepts that need to be taken into account when applying the macroeconomic balance framework, especially with respect to the treatment of net factor income payments and transfers.

$$CUR = S - I. \quad (1)$$

The current account balance is explicitly recognized to depend on the real exchange rate, which influences the volumes and prices of exports and imports. A complicating feature is that the effects of changes in the exchange rate on *CUR* usually take some time to materialize fully. *CUR* also depends on the levels of domestic and foreign aggregate demand (or other measures of economic activity) and various other factors.

The broad outline of CGER's approach remains unchanged from the overview presented in Isard and Faruqee (1998) and is recapitulated here for convenience. The first step in applying the framework is to estimate each country's *underlying current account position*, which is the relevant measure of *CUR* for assessing exchange rates from a medium-run perspective. The underlying current account is defined as the value of *CUR* that would emerge at prevailing exchange rates if all countries were producing at their potential output levels and the lagged effects of past exchange rate changes had been fully realized. Under normal assumptions, a country's underlying current account position will be inversely related to the prevailing level of its real exchange rate, as depicted by the negatively sloped line labeled *UCUR* in Figure 4; that is, a decline (or depreciation) in the real exchange rate will normally improve the underlying current account. If the real exchange rate was R_1, the first step in the macroeconomic balance approach would identify the underlying current account position as $UCUR_1$.

The second step is to derive an estimate of each country's *equilibrium saving-investment position*, which is interpreted as a balance that can be regarded as "normal" from a medium-run perspective. Such estimates focus on the right-hand side of equation (1) and also assume that countries are operating at potential output. In Figure 4, the equilibrium saving-investment balance is assumed to be independent of the real exchange rate,[15] as depicted by the vertical *S-I* line.

The third step is to calculate how much real exchange rates would have to change, other things being equal, to be consistent with medium-run fundamentals—that is, to equilibrate, for each country simultaneously, the underlying current account position with the medium-run equilibrium saving-investment balance. Although this calculation is made in a multilateral framework, it is broadly similar to estimating the difference between R_1 and R^*, where R^* corresponds to the medium-run equilibrium exchange rate at which the *UCUR* and *S-I* lines intersect.

The methodology also involves applications of judgment, both in implementing each of the steps in the macroeconomic balance approach and in considering whether and how much to adjust the resulting macroeconomic balance assessments from PPP perspectives and other information that may be relevant. Additional judgment is required in deciding whether the final quantitative assessments imply a need for policy adjustment in the near term or point to significant risks for the macroeconomic outlook.

Underlying Current Account Positions

CGER has focused on two approaches to generating estimates of underlying current account positions. One approach, developed by the IMF's Research Department (RES), is based on a standard trade model that has a relatively simple structure and employs common equation specifications and parameter values across countries (see Appendix II). The model implicitly treats all current account outflows (inflows) as merchandise exports (imports); treats goods produced in different countries as imperfect substitutes;[16] assumes that export (import) volumes depend on both the level of foreign (domestic) activity and the current and lagged values of the real effective exchange rate; and assumes that exchange rate changes are fully passed through into import prices, with no effect on (domestic-currency-denominated) export prices. The model-based estimates of underlying current accounts have the positive attributes of global consistency and transparency, but the aggregation of non-oil trade, oil trade, and other current account items (investment income flows and transfers) and the lack of country-specific detail are disadvantages.

A second approach is based on the current account projections generated by the IMF's country experts in connection with the World Economic Outlook exer-

[15]This simplifying assumption is consistent with the fact that most empirically estimated reduced-form models of industrial country saving and investment behavior do not include the exchange rate among the main determinants. As elaborated below, it is also associated with an assumption that the industrial countries have perfect access to international capital markets (apart from any time-invariant interest rate premia). A more complete macroeconomic framework could recognize that exchange rates may influence saving and investment through their effects on the terms of trade, the profitability of the traded-goods sector (or subsectors susceptible to "Dutch disease"), the level of potential output, and the distribution of income.

[16]As an alternative to treating the goods of different countries as imperfect substitutes, which is the standard approach in models used for projecting trade volumes empirically, some conceptual models distinguish between tradable and nontradable goods, assume that tradable goods are homogeneous across countries, and model current account adjustment as a process of shifting the balance between each country's production and absorption of tradable goods; see, for example, Dooley and Isard (1987) and Obstfeld and Rogoff (2000). Attempts to apply the latter approach empirically are typically constrained by the paucity of data that adequately decompose production and absorption into their tradable and nontradable components.

Figure 4. Medium-Run Fundamentals

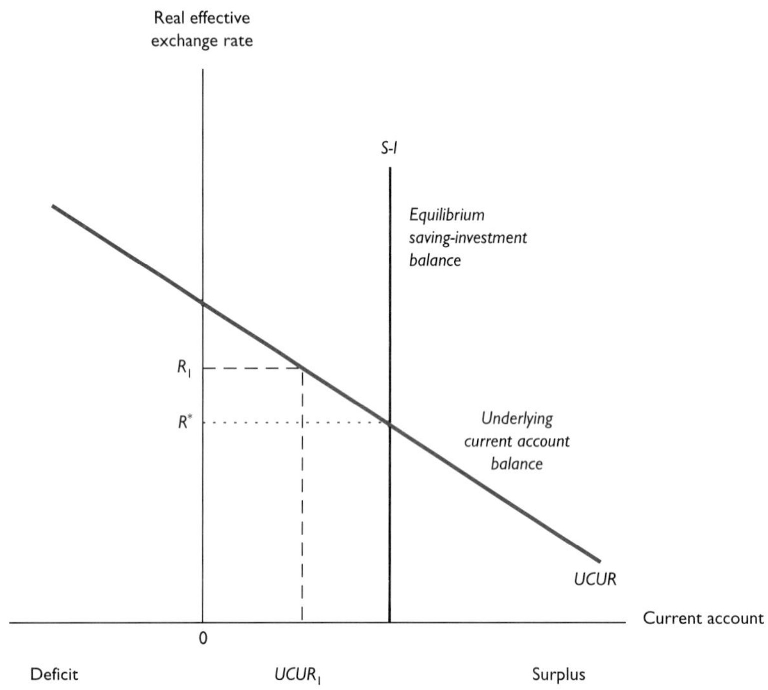

cise. For industrial countries (and most other countries), the WEO projections are conditional on unchanged real exchange rates. Moreover, the projections for the final year in the five-year WEO horizon assume that economies are operating at potential output and, in that sense, can be interpreted as estimates of underlying current account positions. These projections have the advantage of incorporating the country-specific knowledge (including that from models and projections of national authorities) and judgments of the IMF's area department staff. A disadvantage is that the separate projections for individual countries may lack global consistency;[17] indeed, at the time of CGER's semiannual assessment in March 2001, the staff's WEO projections summed to a global current account deficit of 1 percent of projected 2006 world GDP, compared with a global deficit in 2000 of about 0.6 percent of GDP. This global inconsistency, which the WEO forecasts appear to share with most other forecasts, presents a problem for the CGER exercise, as discussed in more detail below.

CGER has chosen to rely primarily on the WEO projections as estimates of underlying current account positions. To avoid relying uncritically on the WEO projections, however, it has disciplined its assessments by generating alternative estimates of underlying current account positions from the globally consistent RES model and taking those estimates into account when shaping its summary judgments on exchange rates. It has also continued to use the RES model in the third step of the CGER process (see below) for calculating the changes in real exchange rates that would be needed to make the underlying current account balances consistent with medium-run equilibrium levels of saving-investment balances.

To strengthen the assessment process, the staff has recently begun to develop benchmarks that can be used as comparators for the individual components of the WEO projections (see Appendix II). The development of these benchmarks amounts, in effect, to an effort to construct an improved version of the RES model that disaggregates the current account into different components and employs a globally consistent and common (across countries) framework for modeling each component.

[17]For major industrial countries, the WEO projections are generated to a large extent from formal models, but the structures of these models differ across countries.

The benchmarks are not intended as an alternative set of projections. The simple analytic models on which they are based, while having the important property of global consistency, do not take account of country-specific factors. Moreover, history reveals considerable variation over time in observed outcomes relative to benchmark calculations for individual countries. Nevertheless, the benchmarks provide CGER with a consistent and disciplined approach for considering the possible directions of bias in estimates of underlying current account balances based on the WEO projections and, accordingly, in the corresponding assessments of exchange rates.

Saving-Investment Norms

The basis for CGER's estimates of equilibrium or normal saving-investment balances, here referred to as *S-I norms*, is an estimated equation generated in the Research Department. This aspect of the present CGER framework remains considerably oversimplified but can be viewed as a significant advance in terms of global consistency.[18]

The assumptions and derivation of the S-I model are described in Appendix III.[19] Updated estimates for the period 1971–99 yield the following long-run relationship:

$$CUR = c_i + 0.23\ SUR + 0.11\ YPCAP, \qquad (2)$$

where *CUR* is the current account (expressed as a ratio to GDP), *SUR* is the fiscal surplus (as a ratio to GDP) relative to the industrial country average, *YPCAP* is income per capita relative to that of the United States, and the c_i are country-specific constant terms.

Several points may be noted about the general structure and interpretation of this equation. First, current account positions would not change if all countries were to reduce their fiscal positions equiproportionately, or to experience the same rates of per capita income growth. Second, the use of the equation to estimate the medium-run equilibrium levels of saving-investment balances relates the S-I norms to structural fiscal positions and cyclically adjusted levels of relative per capita incomes, since the calculations are based on projections at the end of the WEO horizon, where output gaps are zero. Third, the structural fiscal positions that enter the S-I norms do not necessarily correspond to "desirable" fiscal balances; nor should connotations of desirability be attached to the equilibrium or "historically normal" S-I balances.

As elaborated in Appendix III, the long-run relationship described by equation (2) is derived from a model that takes account of cyclical variables, but country-specific interest rates play no explicit role. Accordingly, the present version of the S-I model abstracts from various factors that are relevant to capital flows and portfolio allocation decisions in a world in which claims on different countries are perceived to offer different expected returns and to be subject to different risks.[20] Future efforts to strengthen the S-I model should attempt to capture the influence of such factors, but hopes for major improvements in this area are dimmed by the fact that economists have not yet had much success in empirical efforts to explain how such factors systematically influence the behavior of country-specific interest rate premia.

The parameter estimates in equation (2) imply that a 1 percentage point of GDP increase in a country's *relative* structural fiscal surplus improves its current account by 0.23 percentage points of GDP. Changes in fiscal positions are thus found to have "non-Ricardian" effects; that is, an increase in public saving is not fully offset by a reduction in private saving.[21] A 1 percent improvement in a country's relative per capita income raises its saving-investment balance by 0.11 percentage points of GDP, consistent with the view that higher-income countries tend to be larger (net) exporters of capital, other things being equal. The framework implicitly captures the countercyclical effects of monetary policy on the output gap, which is included in the estimated equation (see Appendix III), but abstracts from any explicit influence of monetary policy on the medium-run behavior of S-I balances or real exchange rates.[22]

[18]Polak (1995) points to the lack of agreed analytic procedures for modeling equilibrium current account positions as a major weakness in the IMF's applications of the macroeconomic balance approach during the 1970s and 1980s. Prior to the estimation of a model of saving-investment behavior over the medium run, CGER's macroeconomic balance assessments for the major currencies were based on ad hoc assumptions about equilibrium ratios of net foreign assets to GDP and associated equilibrium ratios of current accounts to GDP. See Williamson and Mahar (1998) for an alternative exercise in generating S-I norms.

[19]The original econometric estimates are described in Debelle and Faruqee (1996) and Faruqee and Debelle (1998), and the conceptual framework is further elaborated in Masson (1998) and Faruqee, Isard, and Masson (1999).

[20]An implicit assumption is that each country can borrow or lend any amount of capital internationally (i.e., any shortfall or excess of domestic saving relative to domestic investment) at a fixed premium above the world rate of interest. This assumption of perfect capital mobility may be an acceptable simplification for industrial countries but would be inappropriate for most other economies.

[21]There is a long-standing debate on the economic implications of public deficits; see Barro (1989) and Bernheim (1989) for reviews of the Ricardian and neoclassical perspectives.

[22]To the extent that success in mitigating macroeconomic instability tends to promote per capita income growth (and perhaps reduces the cost of servicing public debt) over the medium run, the framework can be viewed to indirectly capture certain longer-run effects of monetary policy.

The saving-investment model has been estimated with country-specific constant terms to capture the effects of omitted variables that may influence the relative saving and investment rates of different countries. These constant terms capture, for example, the fact that a relatively low S-I balance has been historically normal for the United States, other things being equal, consistent with a relatively low observed saving rate for the United States, and perhaps also indicating a relatively strong desire of nonresidents to accumulate claims on the United States.

Equation (2) is a reduced-form relationship and should be interpreted carefully. The relative structural fiscal positions that appear on the right-hand side of the equation should not be regarded as exogenous; in addition to reflecting tax rates and expenditure levels that might reasonably be treated as exogenous, structural fiscal positions can be influenced substantially by factors that affect productivity growth and the level of potential output. Accordingly, changes over time in the relative importance of such factors can make the reduced-form parameters sensitive to the sample period over which they are estimated. It is also widely recognized that the effects of fiscal policy changes on the overall S-I balance can depend (both in magnitude and in sign) on how the policy changes affect perceptions about debt sustainability and the outlook for macroeconomic growth. Further work to better capture the effects of fiscal policy changes on overall saving-investment positions is an important direction for enriching the S-I model.

Although equation (2) is highly simplified and leaves considerable scope for improvement through future research efforts, it provides a consistent way of capturing the sensitivity of overall saving-investment balances to relative fiscal positions, stages of development (per capita incomes), and other unspecified factors operating through the country-specific constant terms. It can be regarded as a formula for generating estimates of equilibrium medium-run current account positions by adjusting historical averages—as captured by the country-specific constant terms—to account for changes over time in variables that one might reasonably expect to affect saving-investment balances. The estimated model has served the important purpose of providing a basis for pinning down a set of judgments on equilibrium saving-investment balances and maintaining a high degree of consistency in those judgments over time. Extensions of the model that succeeded in capturing the influence of additional explanatory variables would also result in different estimates of the country-specific constant terms. Such extensions would affect the time profiles of the S-I norms as functions of the explanatory variables, but they would not affect the historical average levels of the S-I norms, which are determined by observed data. Moreover, to the extent that moving to a more sophisticated model significantly changed the calculated values of the norms for the particular year on which the assessments were based (i.e., the final year of the WEO horizon), discontinuities in the assessments could be avoided—where warranted in CGER's judgment—by making adjustments to the country-specific constant terms.

Figure 5 shows the S-I norms that are implied by equation (2) for the period from 1990 through 2006. The estimates for 2001–06 reflect the WEO projections of explanatory variables as of March 2001. The United States, the United Kingdom, Canada, Australia, and New Zealand are countries in which current accounts have on average been in deficit over the past three decades, which is reflected in the deficit positions of their S-I norms. The other industrial counties are all estimated to have equilibrium S-I surpluses. In the cases of Australia, New Zealand, and Canada, the historically normal deficits in their S-I balances presumably reflect the combined influence of relatively abundant natural-resource-based investment opportunities and relatively sparse populations. The largest surplus norms are associated with Norway and Switzerland, consistent with the effects on S-I balances of substantial oil wealth in the case of Norway and a relatively large net foreign asset position in the case of Switzerland.[23]

The changes in the norms from one year to the next, as derived from equation (2), stem from changes in the observed or projected levels of structural fiscal balances and potential output (cyclically adjusted income) per capita. In the United States the gradual upward trend (decline in the norm deficit) during the 1990s mainly reflects an improvement in the public sector's structural budget position. In Japan the time

[23]The norms reflect adjustments to the country-specific constant terms for Japan, Australia, Denmark, New Zealand, Norway, and Switzerland. In each case, the adjustment has raised the level of the curve shown in Figure 5 without affecting the time profile of the norm; the implicit counterpart of these adjustments is an increase in the size of the deficit norm for the developing countries. For Japan, the norm has been adjusted upward to offset the influence on the estimated country-specific constant term of the abnormal component of investment during the bubble of the 1980s and early 1990s. For Norway, the norm has been judgmentally raised in light of the effects on national wealth and saving of the general rise in oil prices since the historical sample period. For Switzerland, the norm has been judgmentally raised to better capture the implications of a relatively high net foreign asset position. For Australia, Denmark, and New Zealand, the norms were judgmentally raised (to a higher surplus for Denmark and lower deficits in the other two cases) to avoid discontinuities on the occasion of shifting the calculations to updated estimates of the S-I equation.

profile of the norm reflects the widening of the relative structural fiscal deficit[24] and relatively slow growth of potential output during the 1990s, along with the projection for a gradual reduction in the structural fiscal deficit during the five years ahead. For the euro area, the norm has been constructed by aggregating estimates for the individual member countries, with an adjustment to account for temporary effects of German unification in the early 1990s.[25] For most of the other countries, except Switzerland, the variation in the norms primarily arises from changes over time in relative structural fiscal balances. For Switzerland, the downward trend in the norm mainly comes from the relatively slow growth of potential output per capita.

The simple structure of the equation used to calculate the S-I norms is one of the reasons that CGER's assessments should be viewed as imprecise.[26] This poses a challenge for IMF staff in continuing their efforts to generate improved econometric estimates of S-I behavior for the industrial countries in general and to take account of specific factors or structural changes that may have major influences on S-I behavior in individual countries.[27] It bears repeating, however, that the general levels of the S-I norms reflect the average historical values of the S-I balances and would probably not be affected substantially by more sophisticated explanations of the observed data. Thus, the main message that emerges from recent CGER assessments—that the U.S. dollar is considerably stronger than its medium-run equilibrium level—would probably not be altered substantially by a more sophisticated explanation of the historical behavior of the S-I balance for the United States.[28]

Multilateral Exchange Rate Calculations

Step three of the process calculates the direction and magnitude of the implied exchange rate changes that, assuming no changes in policies or other variables, would bring currency values into line with medium-term fundamentals. This section highlights aspects of the analytical framework that are relevant for the interpretation of these calculations and also describes the treatment of the global discrepancy.

As noted above, the *UCUR* line in Figure 4 is negatively sloped to reflect the presumption that a lower real effective exchange rate is associated with an improvement in the current account over the medium term. In the logic of CGER's WEO-based assessments, the position of the *UCUR* line is assumed to reflect the projected values of economic variables at the end of the five-year WEO horizon, when output is at potential and the lagged effects of past exchange rate changes have been realized. Thus, *projected* changes in economic fundamentals, including effects of announced policy changes, are already reflected in the position of the *UCUR* line. By contrast, any *unanticipated* changes in relevant economic variables over the WEO horizon, including changes that arise from unanticipated policy actions, would shift the position of the *UCUR* line.

The vertical *S-I* line in Figure 4 shows the normal level of the saving-investment balance determined in step two. The line is vertical because the normal level of the *S-I* balance (at potential output) is assumed not to depend on the exchange rate.[29] Its position, like that of the *UCUR* line, reflects the projections for relevant economic variables (in this case, per capita income levels and structural fiscal balances) at the end of the medium-run WEO horizon.

Given the initial real exchange rate (R_1) and underlying current account position ($UCUR_1$), the amount of exchange rate adjustment that is needed to equili-

[24]The deterioration of Japan's *relative* structural fiscal deficit during the 1990s stems from both the substantial deterioration of Japan's own fiscal position and significant improvements in structural fiscal positions elsewhere.

[25]The panel data set used to estimate the S-I model included the members of the euro area as individual countries, partly in recognition of the separate status of their currencies during most of the sample period and also to provide more degrees of freedom. Aggregate euro area variables were then constructed either by adding the variables for the individual member countries or as weighted averages, as appropriate. (Weighted averages make sense for variables expressed as ratios to GDP, including the country-specific constant terms in the equation that explains the S-I balance as a ratio to GDP.) For purposes of using the RES model to calculate the amounts that current accounts and exchange rates need to adjust to reach medium-run equilibrium levels (see below), intra-euro-area trade was removed from measures of euro area exports and imports. This makes the framework consistent with the assumption that adjustments in euro exchange rates affect trade between the euro area and the rest of the world but do not affect trade among members of the euro area. It also has the effect of treating the euro area in the aggregate as a less open economy than its individual member countries on average.

[26]Such oversimplification limits the usefulness of the macroeconomic balance approach as a normative tool, just as the usefulness of a PPP-based assessment for normative purposes is limited by sensitivity to the type of price index and averaging period chosen.

[27]Krajnyák (2000) has developed a portfolio allocation model of S-I behavior for Switzerland.

[28]As elaborated in Appendix III, the estimates of the S-I model were updated prior to the March 2001 assessment exercise, which changed the 2006 value of the calculated S-I norm for the United States to a deficit of 1.6 percentage points of GDP—an upward revision (in absolute value) of ¾ of 1 percentage point of GDP. That reduced by about 10 percentage points the macroeconomic balance calculation of the amount that the U.S. dollar would need to depreciate in multilateral terms to reach its medium-run equilibrium level.

[29]As noted earlier, this simplifying assumption could be relaxed in principle (implying a nonvertical *S-I* line)—for example, to recognize the phenomenon of "Dutch disease." However, the simplifying assumption is consistent with many other empirical models of saving and investment behavior.

Figure 5. Saving-Investment Norms, 1990–2006
(In percent of GDP)

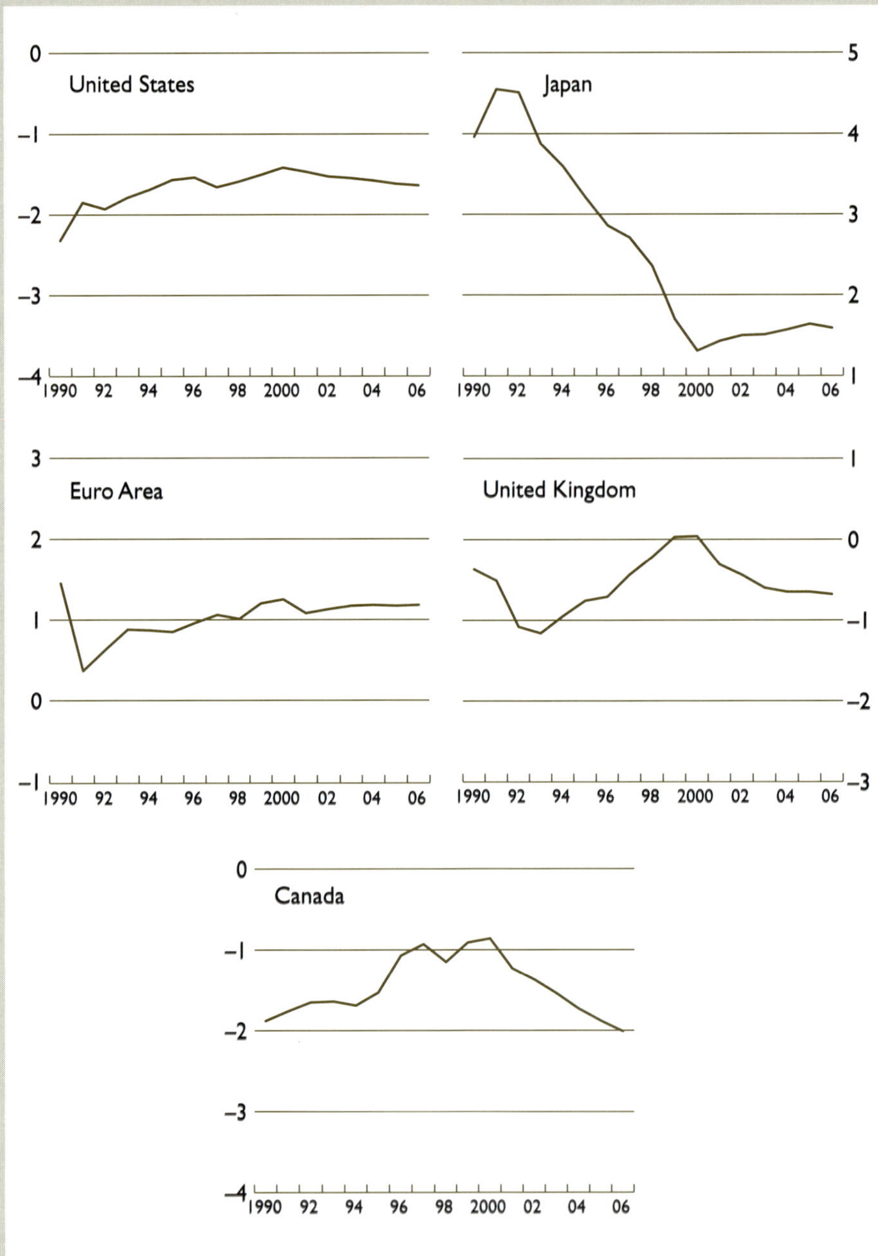

brate the underlying current account with the equilibrium *S-I* balance depends on the slope of the *UCUR* line. The assumptions on which the calculations are based (see below) imply that the slope of the *UCUR* line depends on the openness of the economy. Countries with relatively high ratios of exports and imports to GDP have relatively flat *UCUR* lines and require smaller percentage changes in their real exchange rates, other things being equal, to achieve given changes in their trade volumes or underlying current account positions (as shares of GDP).

Unexpected changes in economic fundamentals—that is, deviations from the changes projected in the WEO—can shift the position of either the vertical

Figure 5 *(concluded)*

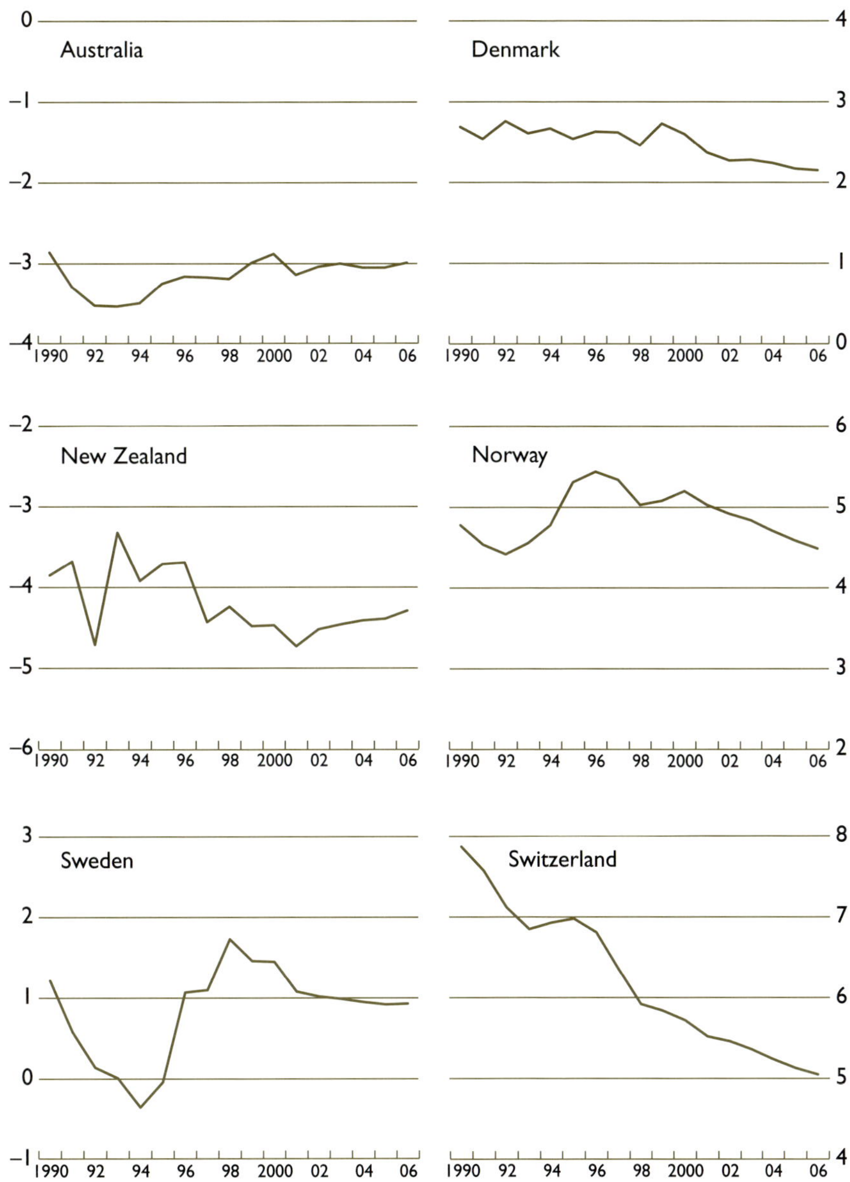

Source: IMF staff estimates.

S-I line or the negatively sloped *UCUR* line or both, and can thereby alter the real effective exchange rate that is consistent with medium-run fundamentals. For example, a greater-than-projected increase in (relative) per capita income or the (relative) structural fiscal surplus will shift the *S-I* line in Figure 4 to the right. The size of the implied change in the equilibrium exchange rate will depend on the extent of the shift in the vertical *S-I* line, on the slope of the *UCUR* line, and on the extent of any shift in the *UCUR* line. By themselves, shifts in the position of the *UCUR* line (due to unexpected changes in medium-run fundamentals that affect the current account through channels other than the real exchange rate) change the equilibrium level of the real effective exchange rate that is consistent with medium-run fundamentals, but they do not change the medium-run levels of either the saving-investment balance (assuming a fixed and vertical *S-I* line) or, correspondingly, the current account balance.

For a more complete picture of how the exchange rate assessments are affected by policy changes or other exogenous shocks, one needs to look behind the *UCUR* line shown in Figure 4. An understanding of how the *UCUR* line shifts requires an understanding of how the shocks affect the WEO projections that CGER relies upon as measures of underlying current account positions. Moreover, in judging the plausibility of the exchange rate assessments, it is important to reflect on the adequacy of the reduced-form *S-I* equation for analyzing the shock under consideration.

This can be illustrated by considering how a permanent reduction in tax rates would affect the equilibrium exchange rate depicted in Figure 4. Equation (2) describes the normal effect on the *S-I* balance; the reduction in the public sector surplus is largely but not completely offset by an increase in the private sector saving-investment balance, with the leftward shift in the *S-I* line (decline in the overall saving-investment balance) tending to raise the equilibrium level of the real exchange rate, other things being equal. But that is only part of the story. In addition, a permanent tax cut would normally lead to upward adjustments in the projections for potential output, absorption, and imports in the medium run, and the associated leftward shift in the *UCUR* line (decline in the projected current account surplus) would tend to lower the equilibrium level of the real exchange rate. Thus, in the normal case the shifts in the *S-I* line and *UCUR* line act in opposite directions on the equilibrium exchange rate. To the extent that the *UCUR* line shifted more than the *S-I* line, the equilibrium exchange rate would decline. In some cases, moreover, the effects on the *S-I* line may differ from the normal response. Just as fiscal consolidation can be expansionary if it eases concerns about debt sustainability and results in reductions in the interest rate premia faced by the country's residents, tax cuts that created strong concerns about debt sustainability could increase precautionary saving, reduce investment, and shift the *S-I* line to the right. In such cases the effect on the equilibrium exchange rate would be unambiguously negative.

As a second example, an increase in a country's per capita income that resulted from a permanent shock to productivity in its tradable goods industries would shift the *S-I* curve to the right. It would also improve the country's international competitiveness (provided that factor costs in the tradables sector rose less than proportionately) and be reflected in a rightward shift of the *UCUR* line. The outcome could well be a higher real effective exchange rate, depending on the balance of the two effects.

In moving from the analysis of the equilibrium level of the real effective exchange rate of a single country, as depicted in Figure 4, to conclusions about the equilibrium configuration of exchange rates in a multicountry world, it needs to be recognized that an n-country world has only $n - 1$ independent exchange rates. It is not feasible to apply Figure 4 independently to all countries (or regions) without imposing a mathematical requirement for global consistency. The general procedure for producing such multilaterally consistent calculations is described elsewhere.[30, 31]

The calculations reflect two sets of specific assumptions. For purposes of characterizing the responsiveness of current account flows (and hence the underlying current account) to changes in real exchange rates, CGER relies on the aggregated RES model described earlier. This model treats each country in the same globally consistent manner, and its parameters have been calibrated to reflect representative estimates from the literature,[32] with the elasticities (per-

[30]See Faruqee (1998). When the sum of the underlying current account positions is reasonably similar to the sum of the saving-investment norms, the results of calculating equilibrium exchange rates in a multilateral framework generally do not deviate materially from those derived by focusing on countries individually (as in Figure 4).

[31]Since the introduction of the euro, CGER has assessed the euro area as a single bloc, effectively reducing the number of currencies that enter its multilateral calculations. The multilateral calculations focus on real exchange rates, and the methodology abstracts from the second-order effects that inflation differentials (and, hence, changes in real exchange rates) within the euro area might have on current account adjustment for the euro area as a whole. Because the euro area as an aggregate is a less open economy than its individual members on average, its consolidation into a single unit can be regarded, in the context of Figure 4, as the substitution of a relatively steep *UCUR* locus for a set of relatively flat *UCUR* lines. A relatively flat *UCUR* line implies that a country's current account has a relatively high responsiveness to a change in its *effective exchange rate* vis-à-vis the currencies of *all* other countries. However, because trade among members of the euro area is a relatively large share of their international trade, the aggregate current account of this group of countries with relatively flat *UCUR* lines and internally fixed exchange rates will not exhibit a relatively high responsiveness to a change in their exchange rates vis-à-vis external currencies. At the time that CGER modified its methodology to incorporate the euro area as a single bloc (early 1999), its assessments under the old methodology did not suggest a need for substantial adjustments of the individual euro legacy currencies vis-à-vis each other. Calculations of the euro's medium-run equilibrium exchange rates under the new methodology differed by about 3 percent from the corresponding estimates for the synthetic euro under the old methodology.

[32]See Goldstein and Khan (1985). The calibrated long-run (and medium-run) elasticity of export (import) volume with respect to the real effective exchange rate is 0.71 (0.92), and it is assumed that exchange rate changes are fully passed through over the medium run into import prices, with no effect on domestic-currency-denominated export prices.

Table 1. Illustrative Assessments

	Underlying Current Account Minus S-I Norm (In percent of GDP)	Multilateral Real Exchange Rate (As percentage deviation from estimated medium-run equilibrium level)[1]	
		Calculated	Summary judgment
	(1)	(2)	(3)
Country A	–2.5	↓ 26	↓ >20
Country B	–2.5	↓ 7	↓ about 10
Country C	0	↑ 4	↑ about 10

[1]↓ indicates that currency would need to depreciate to reach its medium-run equilibrium level; ↑ indicates need to appreciate.

centage responsiveness) of export and import volumes to a given percentage change in the real exchange rate assumed to be identical across countries. Accordingly, in relatively open economies—that is, in countries with relatively high ratios of exports and imports to GDP—a given percentage change in the real exchange rate generates relatively large changes in trade volumes and current account balances as shares of GDP.

The second set of specific assumptions relates to the treatment of the global current account discrepancy. Although the multilateral calculation procedure itself is globally consistent (to a very close approximation), the WEO current account projections for individual countries add up to a global total current account balance that has tended to differ substantially from the sum of the estimated saving-investment norms.

Table 1 illustrates how openness and the global discrepancy influence the multilateral calculations. The table focuses on three countries, with country B representing a much more open economy than countries A and C. For countries A and B, the underlying current account positions are 2½ percentage points of GDP more in deficit (less in surplus) than the equilibrium S-I balances, while for country C the underlying position coincides with the S-I norm (column 1). The calculated estimates of how much prevailing exchange rates deviate from their medium-run equilibrium levels in multilateral or real effective terms (column 2) have two noteworthy features. First, the assessments of multilateral exchange rates for countries A and B are quite different, despite the identical gaps between their underlying current accounts and S-I norms. Second, the exchange rate of country C is assessed as needing to appreciate somewhat to reach its medium-run equilibrium level, despite the fact that the underlying current account of country C is exactly equal to the S-I norm.

Part of the difference between the assessments for countries A and B is explained by the fact that the calculations reflect not only the discrepancies between underlying current accounts and saving-investment norms, but also the different degrees of openness of the two countries. Because country A is a relatively closed economy in comparison with country B, each percentage point of GDP adjustment in the current account requires a larger multilateral exchange rate adjustment in country A. Another part of the explanation, which also pertains to the assessment for country C, is associated with the global discrepancy.

As of early 2001, the WEO projections for individual countries summed to a global current account deficit of $422 billion in 2006, or 1 percent of the projected level of world GDP in 2006, compared with an estimated global discrepancy of –$182 billion in 2000.[33] The average global discrepancy over the past two decades was a deficit of 0.4 percent of GDP, which CGER uses as a norm for the global S-I balance. This historical discrepancy ratio and the WEO projection for global GDP in 2006 implied a global discrepancy of –$168 billion in the S-I norms for 2006.

The large difference between the global discrepancy in the underlying current account positions and the global discrepancy in the S-I norms has a signifi-

[33]Outside forecasts appear to exhibit a broadly similar degree of global export pessimism. In particular, as of April 2001, the Consensus Forecasts, which are based on surveys of more than 200 prominent financial and economic forecasters and extend over a two-year horizon, showed the global current account deficit widening to about –$300 billion in 2001 and –$340 billion in 2002, compared with the WEO projections of about –$260 billion and –$300 billion, respectively.

cant effect on the calculations. If the world as a whole was treated as a single country, a depreciation of 4.4 percent (relative to a hypothetical mirror-image country) would be required, other things being equal, to adjust its current account from the projected aggregate current account deficit ($422 billion) to the deficit level consistent with the historical average global discrepancy ratio ($168 billion). Analogously, independent comparisons of the underlying current account positions and S-I norms for individual countries would tend to suggest estimates of equilibrium exchange rates that were biased by about 4.4 percentage points on average. The mechanical calculation procedure is appropriately constrained to be multilaterally consistent, and it essentially removes the bias in a manner that reduces (increases) by 4.4 percentage points the amount that each currency needs to depreciate (appreciate) in multilateral terms to reach its medium-run equilibrium level, other things being equal. This is why column 2 suggests that the currency of country C needs to appreciate by about 4 percent in multilateral terms. It also explains, together with openness considerations, why country B's estimated deviation from equilibrium is so small in proportion to that of country A.[34]

Given the significant adjustment implemented to remove the global discrepancy bias, as well as the limitations of the models used to generate the estimates of underlying current account positions and saving-investment norms, the exchange rate assessments that emerge from the application of the macroeconomic balance framework should not be regarded as precise. Retrospective applications to episodes that are widely regarded as extreme misalignments of the major currencies during the past two decades (in particular, exchange rates among the U.S. dollar, the Japanese yen, and the deutsche mark in February 1985 and April 1995, and among major European currencies in June–July 1992) would generally have delivered correct signals at the time.[35] Nevertheless, the various sources of imprecision point to both the desirability of continuing efforts to improve the inputs to the calculations, including the global consistency of the WEO projections, and the need to also take other considerations into account in making judgments about equilibrium exchange rates.

Other Relevant Considerations and Summary Judgments

In moving from the macroeconomic balance calculations (Table 1, column 2) to summary judgments about exchange rates,[36] which are expressed as approximations or ranges (column 3), CGER takes account of PPP perspectives. For countries in which deviations of underlying current account balances from S-I norms suggest substantial over- or undervaluation relative to medium-run fundamentals, it is important to ask whether PPP-based perspectives indicate that the country's price or cost competitiveness is substantially weaker or stronger than its historical trend. Given the imprecision of each approach, CGER's confidence in its judgments about currencies is significantly enhanced when both approaches support the same assessment.

The benchmark comparators for the WEO projections (as described earlier and in Appendix II)—which provide perspectives on possible directions of bias in the macroeconomic balance assessments—can also be useful in forming summary judgments. Similarly, it can be useful to consider different sets of PPP-based perspectives; CGER routinely looks at perspectives based on GDP deflators, consumer price indices, and unit labor costs. Other information that CGER considers includes private forecasts of exchange rates and market forward exchange rates; but this information

[34]The uniform 4.4 percentage point "adjustment" is the outcome of taking as given the WEO current account projections for all countries and the saving-investment norms for the industrial countries, and of accepting as plausible the developing country S-I norm that is implied by the assumed norm for the global S-I balance. The methodology does not allow one to *directly* allocate the adjustment for bias in a nonuniform way. It does, however, permit *indirect* allocation via nonuniform adjustments to countries' underlying current accounts or saving-investment norms, which would have nonuniform effects on the estimates of equilibrium exchange rates. As an extreme example, if the U.S. current account deficit projected for 2006 had been reduced by the entire $254 billion difference (as of early 2001) between the global discrepancy in underlying current account positions and the global discrepancy in S-I norms—thereby reducing the projected U.S. current account deficit by 1.9 percentage points of GDP—no uniform adjustment for bias would have been required. Such indirect allocation of the entire adjustment to the United States would have raised considerably (by about 25 percent) the macroeconomic balance estimate of the medium-run equilibrium value of the dollar, although it would not have affected PPP-based assessments of the dollar's overvaluation.

[35]See Isard and Faruqee (1998). The retrospective applications relied on the RES model to generate estimates of underlying current account positions. They suggested that the U.S. dollar was very substantially overvalued against the Japanese yen and the deutsche mark in early 1985 and substantially undervalued against both of the other key currencies in the spring of 1995. They also suggested that the pound and the lira were substantially overvalued against their partner currencies in the Exchange Rate Mechanism in the months prior to the summer 1992 currency crisis, reflecting large underlying current account deficits in the United Kingdom and Italy.

[36]Along with the assessments of multilateral exchange rates, the macroeconomic balance calculations yield globally consistent assessments of bilateral exchange rates (not shown in Table 1), and CGER extends its summary judgments to bilateral rates.

has not played a significant role in CGER's assessments to date.

For the illustrative assessments shown in Table 1, the PPP-based perspectives supported the assessment that the currency of country A was substantially stronger than its medium-run equilibrium level. The PPP-based perspectives (as well as the benchmark WEO comparators) also supported judgments that the currency of country B was somewhat further above its equilibrium level, and that of country C somewhat further below its equilibrium, than the amounts suggested by the macroeconomic balance calculations.

Applications in IMF Surveillance

The main motivation for CGER's assessments of industrial country exchange rates is to identify cases in which currency values appear to be substantially out of line with medium-run macroeconomic fundamentals. The identification of such cases and the characterization of how much exchange rates deviate from medium-run equilibrium levels reflect a combination of mechanical calculations and judgment. Starting with its assessments in early 1997, CGER has judged the U.S. dollar to be substantially stronger than its medium-run equilibrium level, based on both macroeconomic balance calculations and PPP-based perspectives. It is clear, however, that CGER would have felt much less confident in drawing that conclusion from the macroeconomic balance calculations in the absence of evidence (based on several different PPP-based perspectives) of a substantial erosion of international price and cost competitiveness. In that sense, it is difficult to separate the influence of the quantitative macroeconomic balance methodology from the role played by price- and cost-competitiveness indicators. Both factors contribute importantly to CGER's assessments, and judgments are involved in weighing them, particularly when they suggest significantly different conclusions.

At times, countries need to make decisions about the precise values at which to set nominal exchange rates. This was the case when the Italian lira rejoined the European Exchange Rate Mechanism in 1996, and when decisions were made about the rates at which to lock the euro candidate currencies to the euro. While mechanical applications of CGER's macroeconomic balance framework generated point estimates of appropriate exchange rates on those occasions, the IMF staff was cognizant of the imprecision of its estimates and would not have argued with any confidence that those estimates were more appropriate than the rates that the European authorities eventually agreed upon. The IMF's assessments in those cases also reflected the combined influence of mechanical macroeconomic balance calculations, inspection of various price- and cost-competitiveness indicators, and judgment. Had IMF management concluded that the exchange rates under consideration by the European authorities were substantially out of line with medium-run fundamentals, it would have found an appropriate channel for communicating its analysis and conclusions.

As emphasized earlier, the assessment that a currency is substantially out of line with medium-run fundamentals may have different explanations or interpretations. Accordingly, the implications for the IMF's policy advice in the exercise of its multilateral and bilateral surveillance responsibilities depend on the circumstances. One issue is whether prevailing exchange rates are appropriate or helpful from a short-run perspective. This perspective received prominence during much of the 1997–99 period in considering the implications of the relatively strong U.S. dollar and pound sterling when the U.S. and U.K. economies appeared to be at risk of overheating, while Japan and many European economies were relatively weak.

A second issue is whether deviations of exchange rates from their estimated medium-run equilibrium levels signal a need for policy adjustment. In considering this possible interpretation, it is relevant to note that even after policy changes have been proposed by national authorities, market participants may not view implementation of the proposed measures as fully credible. This was the case in Italy during 1995, when a large underlying current account surplus suggested that the lira was undervalued from a medium-run perspective, while large market interest rate premia on lira-denominated assets suggested that the weak lira reflected market concerns that the political process might not deliver the fiscal adjustment that national authorities were seeking. After the fiscal adjustment was legislated and the political uncertainty was resolved, the lira appreciated to a level that appeared to be broadly consistent with medium-run fundamentals, and in late 1996 Italy rejoined the European Exchange Rate Mechanism.

In some circumstances, adjustment of exchange rates toward estimated medium-run equilibrium levels would appear to be helpful from a cyclical perspective. This was judged to be the case in the spring of 1995, when the U.S. dollar was weak relative to the Japanese yen and the deutsche mark and the U.S. economy seemed at risk of overheating, while the Japanese and European economies were weakening. In those circumstances, the staff and management of the IMF pushed for coordinated interest rate actions by United States, Japan, and Germany, reinforced by medium-term fiscal adjustment in the United States and Europe and market opening measures in Japan.[37] Such proposals for policy adjustments were aimed primarily at moving the economies toward internal balance and, secondarily, at bringing exchange rates into better international alignment. In the event, while monetary policy was eased in Germany and Japan in response to weakening cyclical conditions, the case for higher interest rates in the United States was subsequently eroded by signs of a greater-than-expected slowdown in activity (partly because of spillovers from the economic crisis in Mexico), setting in motion a lowering of U.S. interest rates from early July.

In still other circumstances, deviations of exchange rates from their estimated medium-run equilibrium levels may create concerns at times when prevailing interest rate levels are appropriate for the needs of the domestic economy. Such circumstances raise the question whether policy authorities should attempt to influence market perceptions through foreign exchange intervention or public pronouncements.

[37]See Kahn and Nord (1998) and IMF News Brief No. 95/12, April 14, 1995.

These examples indicate that the quantitative estimates that emerge from CGER's analysis can only be regarded as the starting point for judgmental assessments of how to interpret cases in which exchange rates appear to deviate substantially from their medium-run equilibrium levels. Such deviations can have a range of different interpretations and policy implications and need to be considered on a case-by-case basis.

In addition to considering whether any near-term policy actions might be called for when exchange rates appear to deviate substantially from their medium-run equilibrium levels, it can be important to consider the risks to national economic performances and the global macroeconomic outlook. Although substantial deviations from equilibrium do not necessarily imply a high probability of sudden and sharp corrections, an analysis of what such corrections might imply is an integral part of the exercise of the IMF's multilateral surveillance responsibilities. In that connection, the World Economic Outlook has paid considerable attention in recent years to addressing the possible implications of a sudden and sharp depreciation of the U.S. dollar.

III A Methodology for Assessments of Emerging Market Economies

Points of Departure

The experience of the 1990s has demonstrated that currency and financial sector crises in emerging market economies can have devastating implications for these economies and major spillover effects for the global economy. In response, the IMF has been substantially strengthening its efforts to monitor and address financial sector weaknesses and deficiencies in the provision of transparent data. The buildup of unsustainable balance sheet positions can leave countries vulnerable to sudden declines in capital inflows that make it impossible to sustain current accounts and exchange rates at prevailing levels. The IMF staff has also devoted considerable research to developing a system for monitoring early warning signals of crises.[38]

While CGER's work on emerging market economies will also contribute to vulnerability analysis, it differs from the work on early warning systems (EWS). The latter focuses on models that relate the probability of currency and financial sector crises to a broad set of indicators. Some EWS models have found that crisis probabilities are positively related to variables such as current account imbalances and measures of real exchange rate overvaluation relative to trend. By contrast, CGER's present focus is limited to the current account balance—that is, to only one of the key leading indicators of crises. The current account position is a central consideration in IMF surveillance, and CGER's objective is to develop a more systematic approach for assessing when current account imbalances are a source of vulnerability. While this present effort contributes to assessing the sustainability of pegged exchange rates and, more broadly (including under floating regimes), the likelihood that exchange market pressures could intensify, it is not aimed at this stage at generating quantitative estimates of equilibrium exchange rates for emerging market economies.

[38]For background on the staff's work on early warning systems, see Berg and others (1999).

As in CGER's analysis of industrial countries, the work on emerging market economies has a medium-run orientation. The objective of the industrial country analysis is to form judgments about how much saving-investment balances and exchange rates deviate from the levels toward which they are likely to be pushed by medium-run macroeconomic fundamentals. There is no presumption that CGER can explain the short-run behavior of exchange rates. In a similar spirit, the work on emerging market economies is oriented toward assessing whether current account positions are sustainable over the medium run. Analysis of the sustainability of current account positions from a medium-run perspective can contribute to assessing vulnerability to currency crises in the short run, but CGER's efforts are not focused on providing estimates of crisis probabilities.

CGER's methodology for assessing the current account positions and exchange rates of industrial countries rests on assumptions and simplifications that are not entirely appropriate for most other countries. One of the simplifications that underpins the model of saving-investment behavior for the industrial countries is the implicit assumption that each country can borrow or lend an unlimited amount of capital internationally at a constant premium above the world rate of interest. This assumption facilitates the estimation of the saving-investment equation and is regarded as an acceptable simplification for the industrial countries, but it is not valid for emerging market economies, which generally confront much more limited and variable access to international capital markets, along with changing interest rate premiums.

In addition, the industrial country methodology does not go very far in modeling the linkages between equilibrium saving-investment positions and structural policies. In terms of the earlier discussion of Figure 4, the industrial country methodology pays little attention to the role that structural adjustments can play in shifting the position of the *S-I* line.[39] As a

[39]This reflects the general state of the empirical literature on saving and investment behavior, which has not achieved much success in linking movements in S-I balances to structural changes.

result, it characterizes the equilibrium levels of exchange rates as largely independent of structural policies and, correspondingly, the potential for trade-offs between exchange rate adjustment and structural reforms is absent.

Moreover, although the industrial country framework does explicitly recognize that the need for exchange rate adjustment over the medium run depends on the extent to which structural fiscal positions are adjusted, it assumes that the national saving-investment balance is positively and linearly correlated with the structural fiscal position. This assumption is implicitly based in turn on the assumption of an unchanged interest rate premium, which may not be valid in cases of relatively large adjustments in structural fiscal positions. In particular, a relatively large fiscal contraction (expansion) that improves (worsens) a country's structural fiscal balance may substantially affect market expectations about the sustainability of the country's macroeconomic policies, leading to a significant reduction (increase) in its interest rate premium along with an increase (decrease) in investment relative to saving and, hence, a decline (rise) in the S-I balance. This channel is likely to be more significant in emerging market economies than in industrial countries, although it has also been germane for some industrial countries at times (e.g., Italy).

Because of these considerations and other difficulties,[40] CGER has made only modest progress in developing a framework for emerging market economies. To date its focus has been on developing criteria for assessing the sustainability of current account imbalances. No single criterion for assessing sustainability has been found acceptable; therefore, CGER has developed several criteria to use collectively for identifying countries in which sustainability questions could arise. In addition, because the assessments rely on the WEO projections as estimates of prospective current account positions, CGER has also been developing benchmarks—analogous in purpose to those described earlier for the industrial countries—to provide a consistent and disciplined mechanism for considering possible bias in the WEO projections and, accordingly, in the corresponding assessments of current account sustainability.

Criteria for Assessing Sustainability

As the first step in the effort to extend its framework to emerging market economies, CGER investigated the historical relationship between current account balances and a set of potentially important determinants of medium-run saving-investment positions. This study, conducted by Chinn and Prasad (2000), built on CGER's earlier analysis of the saving-investment behavior of industrial countries; Appendix IV summarizes the econometric methodology and results. While the S-I norms derived from the analysis seem reasonable in many cases, for a number of countries the calculations are more doubtful as estimates of equilibrium saving-investment balances. Such findings imply that despite the relative sophistication of the Chinn-Prasad (CP) effort, it would not be appropriate to base assessments of current account sustainability solely on the CP estimates. It is important to recognize not only the general difficulties that can arise in seeking to explain history with econometric models, but also that history may have limited relevance for the future in individual countries that have undertaken major structural reforms and/or experienced major changes in their access to international capital markets.

This conclusion has led CGER to consider other criteria that can be used in combination with the CP norms—including criteria that focus on ratios of net foreign liabilities (NFL) to GDP.[41] Different criteria may be appropriate for assessing projected current account deficits and projected surpluses. Three additional criteria have been tentatively adopted for assessing whether underlying current account deficits are unsustainably large. These criteria focus on whether projected current account deficits (as ratios to GDP) either exceed the average experience over a recent historical period, or would imply an increase in NFL/GDP from its current level, or would be inconsistent with keeping NFL/GDP below some threshold level over the long run.

Such criteria involve ad hoc choices of the recent historical period (e.g., the past decade) and the threshold NFL/GDP ratio (e.g., that corresponding

[40]The definition and measurement of internal balance or potential output poses greater difficulties in applications to emerging market economies than in applications to industrial countries, and applications to emerging market economies also call for greater attention to the commodity composition of trade and the role of official financing.

[41]In practice, the measurement of NFL/GDP ratios poses several difficulties—in particular, the difficulty of revaluing asset and liability stocks to account for changes in exchange rates and the question of whether to include capital that has flown offshore in a country's stock of foreign assets. Reported data on international investment positions are not available for many developing countries and do not extend back very far where they are available. In addition, these data are based on national sources that employ a variety of methodologies in calculating the values of foreign asset and liability stocks. The data set used by CGER has been assembled and analyzed by Lane and Milesi-Ferretti (2001a, 2001c) and represents the most comprehensive effort to date to construct NFL data based on a uniform methodology. Since that data set ends in 1998, it was extended by cumulating current accounts for 1999–2000 and adding them to NFL stocks at the end of 1998. Measurement error in official current account data, especially in recent years, remains a potential problem with these estimates.

to the seventy-fifth percentile for the sample of emerging market countries). In addition, they abstract from additional considerations that are relevant in assessing current account sustainability, such as the extent to which a country's external liabilities have been built up through foreign direct investment and the maturity and currency composition of its external debt. In light of these considerations, the criteria may well be modified and extended over time as CGER gains experience in applying them. Although the objective is to develop a methodology that can be applied systematically and consistently across countries, it would be inappropriate to presume that large current account deficits should always be resisted, or to lose sight of the potential for capital inflows to make substantial contributions to economic development.

The limitations of the individual sustainability criteria provide the motivation for applying them collectively. For the reasons just discussed, however, it would not be appropriate to draw mechanical conclusions from their application. It is important to take account of the relative heterogeneity of the emerging market economies and to incorporate case-by-case judgments into the assessments. For those countries for which the methodology suggests that current accounts may be unsustainable over the medium run, it is important to consider relevant information that might have been overlooked or distorted in the application of the criteria.[42] The process should also consider whether there are countries not identified by the criteria that might nevertheless be cases in which sustainability issues warrant concern.

[42]It should be recognized, for example, that in countries with IMF-supported programs, policy regimes and economic structure generally undergo substantial changes that tend to be reflected in the WEO projections but may be inadequately taken into account by the criteria for assessing current account sustainability.

IV Summary and Concluding Comments

The primary motivation for the work of the Coordinating Group on Exchange Rate Issues is to identify cases where exchange rates appear to be substantially out of line with medium-run macroeconomic fundamentals. It is recognized that such situations can have different interpretations, depending on the cyclical positions of economies and other circumstances. Whether policymakers should take actions or make pronouncements when the methodology identifies possible misalignments is left as an open question, to be addressed on a case-by-case basis and in the context of considering the extent to which monetary, fiscal, and other policies are appropriate from a broader perspective.

CGER's analysis, which has concentrated to date on industrial country currencies, has helped to form the basis for views expressed to national authorities[43] and in international fora such as the Group of Seven. In keeping with guidance from the IMF Executive Board, CGER's work has not been aimed at providing regular public assessments of currency alignments. On a number of occasions, however, CGER's assessments have underpinned statements by the IMF's staff and management expressing qualitative judgments about exchange rates among the major currencies, including in the World Economic Outlook exercise; and in some cases such assessments have appeared in published staff reports.

The assessments of exchange rates among industrial country currencies rely primarily on an application of a macroeconomic balance framework. This framework focuses on the extent to which the current account positions associated with prevailing exchange rates are consistent with medium-run fundamentals. CGER's assessments also take account of purchasing power parity considerations, which provide perspectives on how much exchange rates deviate from historical trends in real terms (i.e., after adjusting for inflation). The formal analysis provides a starting point for a more judgmental assessment of the appropriateness of prevailing exchange rates in the context of a wider range of considerations, including the cyclical positions of national economies.

The macroeconomic balance methodology is based on comparisons of underlying current account positions with estimates of medium-run "equilibrium" saving-investment balances. The underlying positions are the external balances that would emerge at prevailing exchange rates if all countries were operating at potential output and the lagged effects of past exchange rate changes had been fully realized. The assessments rely on the WEO projections as measures of these underlying positions. The measures of equilibrium saving-investment balances are derived from an estimated equation, with judgmental adjustments, in some cases, for factors not captured by the equation. Given the estimates of underlying current account positions and equilibrium saving-investment balances, a globally consistent framework is used to calculate the amounts that multilateral and bilateral exchange rates would have to change, other things being equal, to adjust the underlying current account balances to their medium-run equilibrium positions.

CGER's estimates of equilibrium exchange rates are not very precise. Imprecision emerges both from the limitations of the conceptual models and empirical techniques used to generate estimates of underlying current account positions and equilibrium saving-investment balances, and from the need to adjust for global current account discrepancies. Nevertheless, for cases where the assessments point to substantial deviations of exchange rates from their medium-run equilibrium levels, the qualitative findings are noteworthy. Retrospective applications of the CGER methodology to episodes that are widely regarded as extreme misalignments of the major currencies during 1980–95 would generally have delivered correct signals at the time.

Substantial discrepancies between exchange rates and their medium-run equilibrium levels, when they emerge, raise two different but related issues for the IMF to address in its exercise of bilateral and multilateral surveillance. One issue is whether such discrep-

[43]Most staff reports on Article IV consultations with industrial countries outside the euro area, as well as staff reports on consultations with European Union institutions, now include discussions of CGER (or CGER-type) assessments.

ancies imply that policy adjustments are warranted in the near term. A second question is how macroeconomic performance would be affected in the event of a sudden and sharp exchange rate correction.

The analytic framework that CGER uses to assess the current account and exchange rate positions of industrial countries rests on capital mobility assumptions that are not entirely appropriate for most emerging market economies. Accordingly, CGER has been developing an alternative methodology for the emerging market countries, focusing first on criteria for assessing whether their underlying current account deficits or surpluses may be unsustainable. CGER's analysis of the sustainability of current accounts from a medium-run perspective is still at a preliminary stage. Over time, such analysis could contribute to assessing vulnerability to currency crises in the short run and complement ongoing work to develop and implement an early warning system based on a broader set of indicators.

Appendix I Alternative Methodologies for Assessing Equilibrium Exchange Rates

As discussed in Section II, CGER's assessments for the industrial countries rely primarily on the macroeconomic balance framework, while also taking account of traditional purchasing power parity perspectives. In discussing this choice of methodology, it may be useful to consider briefly several approaches on which CGER has chosen not to rely.

Extended Purchasing Power Parity with Balassa-Samuelson Effects

An important modification or refinement of the long-run PPP hypothesis has come from the observation that the prices of nontradable goods and services, relative to the prices of tradables, tend to be higher in high-income countries than in low-income countries. This observation emerged from attempts to make quantitative comparisons of living standards in different countries in a series of projects sponsored by the United Nations and other international organizations, and spearheaded to a large extent by economists from the University of Pennsylvania.[44] These studies have established that the methodology of comparing international standards of living by converting national accounts data at market exchange rates into a common currency unit generally understates the living standards of low-income countries relative to those of high-income countries. Samuelson (1994) has referred to this empirical regularity as the "Penn effect."

Balassa (1964) and Samuelson (1964) attempted to explain the empirical regularity, along with an apparent tendency for market exchange rates to deviate systematically from PPP over the long run. They conjectured that the tendency for the relative price of nontradables to be higher in high-income countries reflected a tendency for productivity in the tradable goods sector to rise relative to productivity in the nontradables sector as real incomes expanded.[45] Given competitive pressures within each country for workers with similar skills to receive similar wages in the two sectors, relatively rapid productivity growth in the tradables sector would tend, other things being equal, to push up the relative cost of production in the nontradables sector and, hence, the relative price of nontradables. Under conditions in which the relative price of tradable goods across countries remained constant, such an increase in the relative price of nontradables would in turn give rise to an appreciation of the real exchange rate.[46]

For purposes of policy analysis, the extended PPP framework provides a basis for refining the traditional PPP formula to take account of trends in the relative prices of nontradables. CGER has not attempted such a refinement, however, partly because PPP considerations play a secondary role in its assessments, partly because its focus has been primarily on the industrial countries, where the case for such refinement is relatively weak, and partly because the prospective gains from such refinement are limited by difficulties in measuring (or finding suitable proxies for) trends in the relative prices of nontradables.[47]

Estimated Reduced-Form Exchange Rate Models

During the decade that followed the breakdown of the Bretton Woods exchange rate system in the early 1970s, international economists devoted considerable attention to the formulation and empirical testing of reduced-form exchange rate models. Contributors to this approach typically started by describing macroeconomic behavior in terms of a small number of key

[44]See, for example, Gilbert and Kravis (1954); Kravis, Heston, and Summers (1982); and Summers and Heston (1991).

[45]Harrod (1939) provided an earlier discussion of some of the key arguments made by Balassa and Samuelson, the seeds of which have been traced back to Ricardo (1821).

[46]See Isard and Symansky (1996) for a formal description of how the PPP formula can be modified to allow for Balassa-Samuelson effects. Like traditional PPP, the extended hypothesis does not provide an empirically valid description of exchange rate behavior in the short run.

[47]Some economists have used GDP per capita as a proxy; see De Broeck and Sløk (2001) and International Monetary Fund (2000), Box 4.4, pp. 168–69.

behavioral relationships and then combined the relationships to arrive at a single reduced-form equation for the exchange rate. These reduced-form models often fit the historically observed data fairly well within the sample periods over which they were estimated. As already noted, however, by the early 1980s a careful evaluation of such results had delivered the sobering assessment that a variety of state-of-the-art single-equation reduced-form models, in forecasting beyond the sample periods over which the models were estimated, were unable to outperform the predictions of a simple random walk model at *short-run* horizons of up to a year or longer.[48] Indeed, this result even obtained when the post-sample model forecasts were based on realized values of the explanatory variables. Among other things, such findings drove home the point that in-sample goodness-of-fit is not a sufficient criterion for evaluating exchange rate models and that post-sample testing is important.

Advances in econometric methodology since the mid-1980s have provided new techniques for seeking to estimate models that capture the *long-run* relationships between exchange rates and other economic fundamentals.[49] This has led to the development of conceptual frameworks that focus simultaneously on long-run equilibrium conditions for both asset stocks and current account flows (more generally, national income account flows).[50]

At the stage of empirical implementation, this approach may also involve the estimation of single-equation reduced-form models.[51] These specifications have several features that limit their attractiveness. One feature is that they do not yield explicit estimates of equilibrium current account positions. This tends to lessen the appeal of the approach, as it is difficult to judge the plausibility of equilibrium exchange rate estimates unless the associated estimates of equilibrium current account positions can be assessed. A second feature of many of these models is that reducing the conceptual framework to an empirically estimable single equation generally involves simplifying assumptions and precludes identifying the parameters of the fully specified conceptual framework. As a result, the end product typically is significantly less informative than the conceptual framework.[52]

General Equilibrium Frameworks

Approaches based on simulations of general equilibrium models lie at the other end of the spectrum from those based on PPP or estimates of single-equation reduced-form models. The attractive feature of general equilibrium approaches is that the analysis is based on more complete models of macroeconomic behavior; by the same token, however, the added complexity can be a drawback.

Obviously, the general equilibrium approach cannot be implemented for a given country until a macroeconomic model has been specified and estimated for that country. In addition, the case for implementing such an approach depends on whether the available models have well-defined and conceptually appealing long-run properties. Some macroeconomic models that have been designed primarily for purposes of short-term forecasting do not have carefully specified long-run properties, which limits their appropriateness for analyzing the long-run relationship between the exchange rate and other economic fundamentals. Moreover, even when appropriate models are available, the resource-intensiveness of the general equilibrium approach may be an impediment to its application, particularly when the exercise involves assessing equilibrium exchange rates for a number of different currencies simultaneously.

The IMF's global macroeconometric model, MULTIMOD, has carefully specified long-run properties, but other features limit its attractiveness for generating estimates of equilibrium exchange rates.[53] These features derive from the fact that

[48]Meese and Rogoff (1983a, 1983b).

[49]The key advances were the introduction of the concept of cointegration by Granger (1981) and Engel and Granger (1987) and the subsequent development of time-series econometrics.

[50]Such conceptual frameworks define the equilibrium levels or timepaths of exchange rates as the levels or paths that give rise to current account flows that are consistent with convergence to long-run asset stock equilibrium. An early contribution to the empirical implementation of these models was made by Faruqee (1995), based on a continuous-time version of the stock-flow consistent framework described by Mussa (1984). More recently, Alberola and others (1999) have extended the methodology further. Goldman Sachs (1996, 1997) has relied on the methodology in providing forecasts for its clients. See MacDonald (1999) and Clark and MacDonald (2000) for perspectives on the literature. See also Edwards (1989, 1994) and Elbadawi (1994) for applications of this methodology to developing countries.

[51]These reduced-form error-correction models, which in some cases are vector-equation frameworks rather than single equations, contain long-run components that embody the PPP hypothesis; in that sense, they can also be viewed as extensions of the traditional PPP hypothesis. In these reduced-form models, however, PPP is embodied not as a time-invariant level of the long-run real exchange rate, but rather as a steady-state condition in which the equilibrium level of the real exchange rate depends on the steady-state levels of various fundamental determinants.

[52]Another difficulty arises from the fact that the models relate trends in real exchange rates to the observed values of other variables. Accordingly, the derived estimates of equilibrium exchange rates are conditional on assumptions about the equilibrium values of explanatory variables; and for some of these explanatory variables, such as ratios of net foreign liabilities to GDP, economists may not have strong prior beliefs about long-run equilibrium values.

[53]See Laxton and others (1998) for a description of MULTIMOD.

MULTIMOD was not designed for purposes of generating a baseline forecast, but was rather intended to analyze the implications of various shocks to the global economy, using as its baseline the medium-term WEO projections, which reflect the detailed knowledge and judgments of the IMF's country economists. The WEO projections are generated for a five-year horizon, and beyond that various assumptions are imposed to extend MULTIMOD's baseline into a model-consistent balanced growth path. As such, MULTIMOD's baseline (or control solution) reflects the assumption that real exchange rates remain constant over the WEO horizon and imposes fairly strong constraints on the paths that exchange rates take beyond the WEO horizon.

For most of the "shock minus control" experiments conducted with MULTIMOD, the simulated effects of the shocks—and their plausibility—reflect the dynamic properties of the model, but are largely independent of the baseline. Using MULTIMOD to solve for equilibrium exchange rate paths, however, would be a different type of exercise than simulating the effects of exogenous shocks, and would not be very meaningful in light of the prior restrictions placed on the baseline paths for real exchange rates.[54]

[54]Meredith (1998) has modified the Japan block of MULTIMOD to develop a framework in which it does appear valid to interpret the solutions for exchange rates as equilibrium paths. This required strong simplifying assumptions, however, and an effort to extend the framework to the other country blocks in MULTIMOD would be a resource-intensive project.

Appendix II A Model of Current Account Adjustment and Benchmark Comparators for the WEO Projections

In applying its macroeconomic balance methodology, CGER relies on WEO projections as its estimates of underlying current account balances. For a number of years CGER also used a simple calibrated trade model developed in the IMF's Research Department to generate alternative estimates of underlying current accounts (see Bayoumi and Faruqee, 1998). This framework—known as the aggregated RES model—employs common equation specifications and parameter values across countries and treats each country's current account outflows as a homogeneous aggregate. Goods (and nonfactor services) produced in different countries are modeled as imperfect substitutes, with export (import) volumes assumed to depend on both the level of foreign (domestic) activity and the current and lagged values of the real effective exchange rate. In addition, the aggregated RES model assumes that exchange rate changes are fully passed through into import prices, with no effect on (domestic-currency-denominated) export prices.

While it was helpful to be able to compare the WEO projections with alternative estimates derived from the aggregated RES model, the two sets of estimates were based on somewhat different concepts of the underlying current account. In particular, the aggregated RES model was designed to yield estimates of what base year current account positions would be if all countries were producing at potential output and after adjusting for the full effects of past exchange rate changes. By contrast, the WEO estimates are projections of five-year-ahead current account positions, conditional on all countries producing at potential output and no further changes in exchange rates.

Over the past year, the Research Department has implemented several changes in the framework of the RES model to make it more useful for identifying cases in which the WEO-based estimates of underlying current account positions might warrant further consideration. In particular, the Research Department has started to develop a more disaggregated framework that can be used to generate benchmark projections for different components of the current account. The effort to extend the RES model is guided by the degree of disaggregation in the WEO projections, which decompose the current account into three components: non-oil trade, oil trade, and other items (i.e., factor income flows and transfers). The extensions that have been made to the RES framework have not altered the long-run responsiveness of current account positions to changes in real exchange rates, and the aggregated RES model continues to be relied upon in the calculations of equilibrium exchange rates.

The first results of this effort are new equations for modeling the volumes of non-oil exports and imports. The new equations:

- model non-oil trade volumes in a manner that is conceptually similar to the approach adopted in the aggregated RES model, but are designed to generate five- or six-year-ahead "projections" with explicit allowance for the effects of trends in activity variables (as distinct from simply allowing for output gaps to close);[55]
- use measures of real absorption (domestic or weighted-average foreign) as activity variables; and
- are specified in terms of levels of trade flows rather than ratios of trade flows to domestic GDP (or absorption), since domestic activity would not be an appropriate scale variable in six-year-ahead projections of export volumes.

The specific forms of the non-oil trade volume equations are:

$$\Delta Q_x = 1.9\Delta A^f - 0.71[0.3\Delta R + 0.35\Delta R_{-1} + 0.15\Delta R_{-2} + 0.1\Delta R_{-3} + 0.05\Delta R_{-4} + 0.05\Delta R_{-5}]$$

$$\Delta Q_M = 2.1\Delta A + 0.92[0.3\Delta R + 0.35\Delta R_{-1} + 0.15\Delta R_{-2} + 0.1\Delta R_{-3} + 0.05\Delta R_{-4} + 0.05\Delta R_{-5}],$$

[55]The six-year-ahead framework reflects the fact that incomplete or very preliminary data for the current year often makes it desirable to use the previous year as the base year when generating the benchmark projections.

where Q_X and Q_M denote the logarithms of export and import volumes, A and A^f denote the logarithms of domestic and foreign real absorption, R is the logarithm of the real exchange rate (with an increase in R representing a real appreciation), and the Δ terms refer to changes over six-year intervals.[56]

The parameter values and lag patterns that describe the responses of trade volumes to changes in real exchange rates are identical to those in the previous specification of the RES model,[57] but the activity elasticities have now been set at 1.9 for non-oil export volumes and 2.1 for non-oil import volumes. This parameterization—with non-oil trade volumes calibrated to grow about twice as fast as economic activity when real exchange rates remain constant—provides a "good fit" to the history of the past 15 years for the industrial countries *on average*.[58] The slight asymmetry between the two elasticities allows for the fact that the trade volume equations focus on a measure of aggregate demand as the sole activity variable, abstracting from supply-side factors that tend to have stronger effects on developing country exports (industrial country imports) than on industrial country exports.[59]

The new trade volume equations provide benchmark comparators for the corresponding components of the WEO projections. The benchmarks are not intended as an alternative set of projections: they do not take account of country-specific factors, and history reveals considerable variation over time in observed outcomes relative to retrospective benchmark calculations for individual countries. Nevertheless, the benchmarks provide CGER with a consistent and disciplined approach for considering the possible bias in the corresponding components of the WEO projections. Although the benchmark calculations take as given the WEO projections for absorption, they identify cases in which the projected changes in trade volumes relative to absorption seem inconsistent with the recent history of exchange rate movements.

In addition to deriving benchmarks for the volumes of non-oil trade flows, CGER has initiated efforts to develop benchmarks for the prices of non-oil exports and imports by modeling these prices in a manner that captures an element of pricing-to-market in the short run while also reflecting the long-run trends in general price levels. It would be desirable, at a later stage, to further extend the benchmarks by modeling oil trade in a systematic manner that captures the sensitivity of oil import (and export) volumes to changes in the relative price of oil, and by systematically linking investment income flows to asset stock positions and the general level of interest rates.

[56]Under the assumption that real exchange rates remain constant at prevailing levels, the square-bracketed terms in the equations—when the dating of ΔR corresponds to the change from the base year to six years later—are equivalent to the expression:

$$[1.0\delta R + 0.7\delta R_{-1} + 0.35\delta R_{-2} + 0.20\delta R_{-3} + 0.10\delta R_{-4} + 0.05\delta R_{-5}],$$

where δR represents the (logarithmic) difference between the real exchange rate on which the WEO projections are conditioned and the average real exchange rate during the base year; δR_{-1} represents the difference between the average real exchange rate in the base year and the average real exchange rate during the previous year; and so forth. The weights on each "incremental" exchange rate change can be interpreted as the proportion of the long-run effect of that change that is yet to be realized.

[57]The framework reported in Bayoumi and Faruqee (1998) was modified at the end of 1998 based on econometric work that supported the shift from a three-year distributed lag to a five-year lag.

[58]An elasticity of 2.5, which would be more consistent with the previous version of the calibrated RES current account model (in which *ratios* of trade volumes to GDP were assumed to exhibit an elasticity of 1.5 with respect to GDP), would show substantially more trade expansion than has been observed historically.

[59]The deviations of these elasticities from 2.0 generate six-year-ahead projections in which the aggregate current account position for the industrial countries is roughly consistent with the industrial country S-I norm. The asymmetry in activity elasticities tends to (partly) offset the trade-balance effects of absorption growing more slowly in industrial countries than in the rest of the world.

Appendix III The Saving-Investment Model for Industrial Countries

The saving-investment (S-I) model relates each country's current account (saving-investment balance) to four explanatory variables: its stage of development, as represented by its per capita income position; its fiscal position; the gap between its actual and potential output levels; and the level of world interest rates. An earlier version of the equation included the ratio of the dependent-age population to the working-age population as a fifth explanatory variable. The conceptual framework is described by Masson (1998). The model is simplified by imposing the constraint that aggregate saving must equal aggregate investment for the world as a whole, which provides a condition that links the level of the world interest rate to the other variables in the model. This condition can be substituted for the level of the world interest rate to derive an equation that relates each country's S-I balance to relative levels of its per capita income, fiscal position, and output gap. Substituting out the world interest rate is not equivalent to treating it as a constant, or as irrelevant to the S-I balances of individual countries, but rather amounts to an implicit assumption that the world interest rate is determined by global variables—including, in particular, global measures of income per capita, the fiscal balance, and the output gap.

Econometric testing of the model focused on both cross-section and panel results, exploring the panel data with both error-correction and partial-adjustment models, taking into consideration a reasonably long list of candidate explanatory variables, and settling in the end on a partial-adjustment equation. The specification had the form:

$$CUR = \mu_i + \lambda CUR_{-1} + \beta_1 SUR + \beta_2 DEM + \beta_3 YPCAP + \beta_4 GAP,$$

where *CUR* is the current account (as a ratio to GDP), *SUR* is the fiscal surplus (as a ratio to GDP) relative to the industrial country average, *DEM* is the dependency ratio relative to the industrial country average, *YPCAP* is income per capita relative to that of a reference country (the United States), *GAP* is the output gap, and the μ_i are country-specific constant terms. The model also included a dummy variable to capture the effects of German unification from 1990 onward.[60]

The econometric results that emerged from the original set of tests are described by Faruqee and Debelle (1998). The relative fiscal position and most of the country-specific constant terms were highly significant, as were the lagged dependent variable and the output gap. The econometric testing found that, for the industrial countries as a group, country-specific interest rates did not have significant effects on S-I balances when the output gap was also included as an explanatory variable. The indirect and limited role that interest rates play in the S-I model—and, more generally, the inadequate attention to factors that explain the relative attractiveness of investing in different countries—is an issue that warrants high priority in future efforts to strengthen CGER's methodology.[61]

The partial-adjustment model described above can be transformed to derive the following long-run (steady-state) specification:

$$CUR = c_i + \gamma_1 SUR + \gamma_2 DEM + \gamma_3 YPCAP,$$

where $c_i = \mu_i/(1-\lambda)$ and $\gamma = \beta/(1-\lambda)$. The transformation reflects the assumption that output gaps vanish in the long run. This specification corresponds to equation (2) in the main text (but retains the demographic variable).

The variables in the S-I model are viewed as direct determinants of saving and investment in the medium run, which are different from the explanatory variables of the standard trade-equation models that are used to generate estimates of underlying current account positions. Although one of the variables in the estimated partial-adjustment equation is the relative output gap, this variable does not appear in the long-run relationship. Its inclusion in the model enables a better overall fit of the historical data and

[60]See Faruqee and Debelle (1998) for details on the adjustment for German unification.

[61]A number of empirical studies have found strong empirical links between current account flows and country-specific interest rates; see, for example, Obstfeld and Rogoff (2000).

Table 2. Saving-Investment Equation for Industrial Countries
(Model: $CUR = \mu_i + \lambda CUR_{-1} + \beta_1 SUR + \beta_2 DEM + \beta_3 YPCAP + \beta_4 GAP$+ German Unification Dummies)

	CUR_{-1}	SUR	DEM	$YPCAP$	GAP	
1. Original estimates	0.660**	0.153**	–0.045	0.045*	–0.251**	$\bar{R}^2 = 0.76$
1971–93[1]	...	0.45	–0.13	0.14	...	D.W. = 1.8
2. Normalized output gap	0.590**	0.132**	–0.049	0.049*	–0.243**	$\bar{R}^2 = 0.72$
1971–93[1]	...	0.32	–0.12	0.12	...	D.W. = 1.7
3. Youth dependency ratio	0.588**	0.131**	–0.076*	0.048*	–0.246**	$\bar{R}^2 = 0.72$
1971–93[1]	...	0.32	–0.18	0.12	...	D.W. = 1.7
4. Extended sample	0.686**	0.078**	0.024	0.036*	–0.238**	$\bar{R}^2 = 0.77$
1971–99[1]	...	0.25	0.076	0.12	...	D.W. = 1.8
5. Extended sample	0.685**	0.073**	...	0.033*	–0.235**	$\bar{R}^2 = 0.77$
1971–99[1]	...	0.23	...	0.11	...	D.W. = 1.8

Note: A *(**) indicates significance at the 10 (5) percent level.
[1]Implied long-run coefficients, derived as $\gamma_i = \beta_i / (1 - \lambda)$.

better estimates of the parameters that capture the effects of the medium-run determinants.

The estimated parameters used to generate the saving-investment norms for industrial countries were updated prior to CGER's March 2001 assessment exercise. The decision to update was motivated in part by the fact that the framework that CGER had been using as a basis for the norms—equations (6.4) and (6.5) in Faruqee and Debelle (1998)—was estimated over the sample period 1971–93, which it had since become possible to extend through 1999. In addition, during the latter part of 1999 a major revision had been made to the historical real GDP data for the United States—the reference country for the relative income variable used in the S-I equation.

The main implications of updating the data are evident from the five sets of equations reported in Table 2. In each case, the table reports the estimated parameters of the dynamic model and the implied estimates of the long-run coefficients; the panel estimates of the country-specific constant terms (fixed effects) are not reported in the table. In addition to exploring the implications of updating the original estimates (case 1), the new regression results (cases 2–5) are based on a normalized measure of the output gap (*GAP*) in which each country's gap is expressed as a deviation from the GDP-weighted industrial country average.[62]

Comparison of cases 1 and 2 in the table isolates the effects of data revisions and normalization of the output gap. The main effect is a reduction in the long-run coefficient on the relative fiscal surplus (*SUR*) from 0.45 to 0.32.[63] Case 3 indicates that replacing the overall dependency ratio with the youth dependency ratio raises the significance of the relative demographic variable (*DEM*) in the 1971–93 sample. Cases 4 and 5 show the effects of extending the sample period through 1999. Note that the fiscal coefficient falls somewhat further but remains highly significant, while dependency ratios (both the overall ratio and the ratio for youths) have negligible coefficients in the extended sample period; hence they are dropped in case 5.

These findings motivated CGER to shift to basing its S-I norms on the results reported for case 5. In doing so, adjustments were made to the country-specific constant terms in cases for which the new norms would otherwise have implied uncomfortably large discontinuities from the norms that were used in the previous semiannual assessment exercise.[64]

Although the long-run S-I equation includes only two explanatory variables—a situation that calls for continuing research efforts—the limitations of the

[62]The output gap is the only country variable that was not normalized in the original estimation work reported by Faruqee and Debelle (1998).

[63]Not normalizing the output gap—that is, using the exact specification in case 1 but with the revised data—would yield an insignificant coefficient (near zero) on income per capita and a long-run fiscal coefficient of 0.36.

[64]The adjustments to the norms are described in a footnote that accompanies the discussion of Figure 5 in the main text. Although the desire to avoid significant discontinuities motivated adjustments in cases for which the previous norms had seemed reasonable, in other cases the primary motivation was to adjust (or restore previous adjustments) for important country-specific considerations that are not adequately captured by the S-I model.

equation should be evaluated with the following considerations in mind. First, while only two significant explanatory variables appear in the long-run equation, the country-specific constant terms are also highly significant, as are the lagged dependent variable and output gap in the dynamic equation; and the latter equation fits the data fairly well. Second, the S-I norms that CGER adopts are not determined by the equation alone; as noted, in some cases judgments have been incorporated into the norms (via adjustments to the country-specific constant terms) to allow for the effects of omitted factors that are not captured by the equation. Third, the exchange rate assessments do not simply reflect the macroeconomic balance estimates but also take account of PPP-based estimates and provide considerable scope for judgment. And fourth, even in its simple form the S-I equation contributes importantly to maintaining the consistency of CGER's assessments by providing an agreed formula for changing the norms systematically (and gradually) over time in association with changes in variables that are perceived to be important determinants of medium-run saving-investment behavior.

Appendix IV An Econometric Study of Saving-Investment Behavior in Developing Economies

The study by Chinn and Prasad (2000) looked for systematic relationships between saving-investment balances and a fairly long list of possible explanatory variables for developing countries, focusing on both cross-section and time-series data. In contrast to CGER's econometric analysis of the saving-investment behavior of the industrial countries, the Chinn-Prasad (CP) study gave emphasis to exploring the relevance of countries' abilities to attract capital from abroad. The objective was to try to find an acceptable way to model the size of the S-I surpluses or deficits that have been historically observed for developing countries, taking into account, inter alia, economic factors that might limit their access to international capital markets.

Table 3 reports some of the regression findings from the CP study. Column 1 shows results for a sample of 71 developing countries, while columns 2–5 show results obtained after separating the sample into the African countries and the developing countries excluding Africa.[65] The regressions focus on explaining the current account to GDP ratio in terms of the variables listed in the rows of the table. The table reports the magnitudes of all coefficients that were estimated to differ significantly from zero, as well as the signs (+ or –) of coefficients that did not differ significantly from zero. The results reported in columns 3 and 5 include the foreign aid/GDP ratio (row 9) among the explanatory variables; the results in columns 1, 2, and 4 do not. Foreign aid receipts have had a significant negative effect on current account balances in Africa, but have not been a significant explanatory variable for the other developing countries as a group.

As was the case in the industrial country regressions reported in the earlier discussion of equation (2), the government budget balance (row 1) has a significant positive effect on the overall saving-investment balance while the dependency ratios (rows 2 and 3) tend to have negative effects on the saving-investment balance. The regression analysis looked for a nonlinear effect of relative per capita income, based on the hypothesis that, at relatively low stages of development, increases in income would tend to improve a country's access to foreign capital while, at advanced stages of development, the correlation between income and the current account would become positive (or less negative). The latter part of the hypothesis reflects the notion that countries at the highest income levels and most advanced stages of development tend to be capital exporters, an implication of the negative relationship between the abundance of existing capital and the marginal returns on additional investments. The hypothesis suggests a positive coefficient on the relative income squared term (row 5) and finds some support from the results in columns 1 and 2.

Among the other variables tested in the regression analysis, financial deepening (as measured by a ratio of broad money to GDP), openness (exports plus imports as a share of GDP), and the initial net foreign asset (NFA) position as a ratio to GDP were found to have significant effects on the current account to GDP ratio (rows 6–8). A priori, the latter two variables were viewed as particularly relevant to a country's ability to attract foreign capital. The finding of a negative correlation between the S-I balance and openness is consistent with the view that a country's ability to attract foreign capital is enhanced by a relatively large capacity to generate export revenues or compress imports for purposes of meeting debt-service payments.

The significant positive correlation between the current account and the initial NFA/GDP ratio does not have a clear interpretation.[66] Several factors may

[65]Because of data limitations (short time series), transition economies were not included in the sample of countries. Regional dummy variables designed to test the extent to which the developing countries can be treated as a homogeneous group proved insignificant for all regions except Africa. A dummy variable for oil-exporting countries was significantly positive in same specifications, but not in the "final specifications" shown in Table 3.

[66]The CP data set covered the period 1971–95, which was broken into nonoverlapping five-year subperiods, with the panel regression analysis focusing on corresponding five-year averages of annual data as a strategy for trying to see through the shorter-run influences on current account behavior. The initial NFA/GDP ratio was then measured as the ratio existing at the beginning of each subperiod.

Table 3. Results of Panel Regressions
(Dependent variable: current account to GDP ratio)

	Developing Countries (1)	Developing Countries Excluding Africa (2)	(3)	African Countries (4)	(5)
1. Government budget balance (ratio to GDP)	0.39***	0.26***	0.18***	0.60***	0.64***
2. Relative dependency ratio (young)	–	–0.06*	–	–	–0.16**
3. Relative dependency ratio (old)	–	–	+	–	–
4. Relative income	–	–	–	0.33*	–0.45**
5. Relative income squared	0.25**	0.27**	+	–0.49*	+
6. Financial deepening	0.04***	0.04**	0.03*	+	+
7. Openness ratio	–0.03**	–0.02*	–	–	+
8. Net foreign asset/GDP ratio	0.04***	0.04***	0.04***	0.04***	0.03*
9. Foreign aid/GDP ratio	...	...	+	...	–0.51***
10. Terms of trade volatility	+	0.03*	+	+	+
11. Average GDP growth	–	–	+	–	–
12. Capital controls (current account)	+	+	+	+	+
13. Capital controls (capital account)	–	–	+	+	+
14. Dummy for oil-exporting countries	+	+	+	+	–
15. Significant time dummies	1981–85	1981–85	1981–85	None	1976–80 1981–85
Adjusted R-squared	0.44	0.45	0.49	0.49	0.59
Number of observations	223	155	142	68	64

Note: Ordinary least squares specifications with dummy variables for each time period. The dependent and independent variables are nonoverlapping five-year averages of the corresponding annual variables, except for NFA/GDP, which is the observed value during the initial year of each five-year period. The symbols *, **, and *** indicate statistical significance at the 10 percent, 5 percent, and 1 percent levels, respectively; + and – indicate the signs of insignificant coefficients.

be contributing to it. One factor is the direct contribution to the current account of the (net) income on the net foreign asset position. It may also be the case that whatever factors determined the relative attractiveness of countries to capital inflows in the past—and hence led to their initial net foreign liability (asset) positions—have continued to explain the relative sizes of their current account positions. Another plausible interpretation of the positive sign is that it is capturing the effect of the NFA/GDP ratio adjusting toward some long-run equilibrium level.[67]

It would be desirable to be able to separate the different channels through which the current account is affected by the initial net foreign asset position.[68] In principle, this could be done by modeling and estimating simultaneously the equilibrium NFA/GDP ratio and the path of adjustment to long-run equilibrium. Such an undertaking, however, is not straightforward. Similarly, the introduction of country-specific interest rates (or cost of capital measures) into the analysis would present challenges: even if adequate data were available, one would have to deal with two-way causality between the current account and the cost of capital.[69]

The plausibility of the CP equation depends not only on the signs, magnitudes, and statistical significance of the individual estimated parameters but also on the implied estimates of historically normal sav-

[67]However, the correlation between the current account and NFA can be either negative or positive during the transition to long-run equilibrium.

[68]Lane and Milesi-Ferretti (2001b) have taken a significant step in this direction by focusing on the trade balance (TB) and the relationship between TB/GDP and NFA/GDP.

[69]Lane and Milesi-Ferretti (2001a) have recently shown that the evolution of NFA positions over the period 1970–98 can be largely explained by shifts in relative output levels, the stock of public debt, and demographic variables, with the latter two factors particularly important for developing countries.

ing-investment balances or "S-I norms."[70] For many of the emerging market economies on which CGER has focused, the implied S-I norms seem reasonable. For a number of others, however, the calculations seem implausible as estimates of equilibrium saving-investment balances.[71]

[70]In calculating S-I norms for future years, it is highly desirable to shift to WEO data (and projections) for the explanatory variables in the CP equation. Overall, the WEO data generally move in line with the corresponding series in the CP data set, but to align the fitted values of the equation (based on WEO data) with the sample period observations it is necessary to introduce country-specific constant terms (or one-time level adjustments) into the calculations. The constant terms have been calibrated to imply mean-zero errors between observed and fitted current-account-to-GDP ratios over the period 1980–95.

[71]A number of factors that seem important in assessing medium-term sustainability—such as political conditions, the role of past defaults, and the climate for and level of foreign direct investment—are precluded from the analysis by the inherent difficulties of quantification or limitations in available data.

References

Alberola, Enrique, Susana G. Cervero, J. Humberto Lopez, and Angel Ubide, 1999, "Global Equilibrium Exchange Rates—Euro, Dollar, 'Ins,' 'Outs,' and Other Major Currencies in a Panel Cointegration Framework," IMF Working Paper No. 99/175, (Washington: International Monetary Fund).

Artus, Jacques, 1978, "Methods of Assessing the Long-Run Equilibrium Value of an Exchange Rate," *Journal of International Economics*, Vol. 8, pp. 277–99.

———, and Malcolm Knight, 1984, *Issues in the Assessment of the Exchange Rates of the Industrial Countries: A Study by the Research Department*, IMF Occasional Paper No. 29 (Washington: International Monetary Fund).

Balassa, Bela, 1964, "The Purchasing-Power Parity Doctrine: A Reappraisal," *Journal of Political Economy*, Vol. 72 (December), pp. 584–96.

Barro, Robert J., 1989, "The Ricardian Approach to Budget Deficits," *Journal of Economic Perspectives*, Vol. 3 (Spring), pp. 37–54.

Bayoumi, Tamim, and Hamid Faruqee, 1998, "A Calibrated Model of the Underlying Current Account," in *Exchange Rate Assessment: Extensions of the Macroeconomic Balance Approach*, IMF Occasional Paper No. 167, ed. by Peter Isard and Hamid Faruqee (Washington: International Monetary Fund).

Berg, Andrew, Eduardo Borensztein, Gian Maria Milesi-Ferretti, and Catherine Pattillo, 1999, *Anticipating Balance of Payments Crises: The Role of Early Warning Systems*, IMF Occasional Paper No. 186 (Washington: International Monetary Fund).

Bernheim, B. Douglas, 1989, "Neoclassical Perspective on Budget Deficits," *Journal of Economic Perspectives*, Vol. 3 (Spring), pp. 55–72.

Breuer, Janice Boucher, 1994, "An Assessment of the Evidence on Purchasing Power Parity," in *Estimating Equilibrium Exchange Rates*, ed. by John Williamson (Washington: Institute for International Economics).

Cassel, Gustav, 1918, "Abnormal Deviations in International Exchanges," *Economic Journal*, Vol. 28, pp. 413–15.

———, 1922, *Money and Foreign Exchange After 1914* (New York: Constable & Co.).

Chinn, Menzie, and Eswar S. Prasad, 2000, "Medium-Term Determinants of Current Accounts in Industrial and Developing Countries: An Empirical Exploration," IMF Working Paper No. 00/46 (Washington: International Monetary Fund).

Clark, Peter B., Leonardo Bartolini, Tamim Bayoumi, and Steven Symansky, 1994, *Exchange Rates and Economic Fundamentals: A Framework for Analysis*, IMF Occasional Paper No. 115 (Washington: International Monetary Fund).

Clark, Peter B., and Ronald MacDonald, 2000, "Filtering the BEER: A Permanent and Transitory Decomposition," IMF Working Paper No. 00/144 (Washington: International Monetary Fund).

Debelle, Guy, and Hamid Faruqee, 1996, "What Determines the Current Account? A Cross-Sectional and Panel Approach," IMF Working Paper No. 96/58 (Washington: International Monetary Fund).

De Broeck, Mark, and Torsten Sløk, 2001, "Interpreting Real Exchange Rate Movements in Transition Economies," IMF Working Paper No. 01/56 (Washington: International Monetary Fund).

Dooley, Michael P. and Peter Isard, 1987, "Country Preferences, Currency Values and Policy Issues," *Journal of Policy Modeling*, Vol. 9 (Spring), pp. 65–81.

Edwards, Sebastian, 1989, *Real Exchange Rates, Devaluation and Adjustment: Exchange Rate Policy in Developing Countries* (Cambridge, Massachusetts: MIT Press).

———, 1994, "Real and Monetary Determinants of Real Exchange Rate Behavior: Theory and Evidence from Developing Countries," in *Estimating Equilibrium Exchange Rates*, ed. by John Williamson (Washington: Institute for International Economics).

Elbadawi, Ibrahim, 1994, "Estimating Long-Run Equilibrium Real Exchange Rates," in *Estimating Equilibrium Exchange Rates*, ed. by John Williamson (Washington: Institute for International Economics).

Engel, Robert F., and C.W. J. Granger, 1987, "Co-integration and Error Correction: Representation, Estimation, and Testing," *Econometrica*, Vol. 55 (March), pp. 251–76.

Faruqee, Hamid, 1995, "Long-Run Determinants of the Real Exchange Rate: A Stock-Flow Perspective," *Staff Papers*, International Monetary Fund, Vol. 42 (March), No. 1, pp. 80–107.

———, 1998, "Methodology for Calculating Equilibrium Exchange Rates and Question of Global Consistency," in *Exchange Rate Assessment: Extensions of the Macroeconomic Balance Approach*, IMF Occasional Paper No. 167, ed. by Peter Isard and Hamid Faruqee (Washington: International Monetary Fund).

———, and Guy Debelle, 1998, "Saving-Investment Balances in Industrial Countries: An Empirical Investigation," in *Exchange Rate Assessment: Extensions of the Macroeconomic Balance Approach*,

IMF Occasional Paper No. 167, ed. by Peter Isard and Hamid Faruqee (Washington: International Monetary Fund).

Faruqee, Hamid, Peter Isard, and Paul R. Masson, 1999, "A Macroeconomic Balance Framework for Estimating Equilibrium Exchange Rates," in *Equilibrium Exchange Rates*, ed. by Ronald MacDonald and Jerome L. Stein (Boston: Kluwer Academic Publishers).

Flood, Robert P., and Mark P. Taylor, 1996, "Exchange Rate Economics: What's Wrong with the Conventional Macro Approach?" in *The Microstructure of Foreign Exchange Markets*, ed. by Jeffrey A. Frankel, Giampaolo Galli, and Alberto Giovannini (Chicago: University of Chicago Press).

Flood, Robert P., and Andrew K. Rose, 1999, "Understanding Exchange Rate Volatility Without the Contrivance of Macroeconomics," *Economic Journal*, Vol. 109, No. 459 (November), pp. F660–72.

Frankel, Jeffrey A., and Andrew K. Rose, 1995, "Empirical Research on Nominal Exchange Rates," in *Handbook of International Economics*, Vol. 3, ed. by Gene M. Grossman and Kenneth Rogoff (Amsterdam: North-Holland).

Froot, Kenneth A., and Kenneth Rogoff, 1995, "Perspectives on PPP and Long-Run Real Exchange Rates," in *Handbook of International Economics*, Vol. 3, ed. by Gene M. Grossman and Kenneth Rogoff (Amsterdam: North-Holland).

Gilbert, Milton, and Irving B. Kravis, 1954, *An International Comparison of National Products and the Purchasing Power of Currencies: A Study of the United States, the United Kingdom, France, Germany, and Italy* (Paris: Organization for European Economic Cooperation).

Goldman Sachs, 1996, *The Foreign Exchange Market* (July).

———, 1997, *The Foreign Exchange Market* (September).

Goldstein, Morris, and Mohsin S. Khan, 1985, "Income and Price Effects in Foreign Trade," in *Handbook of International Economics*, Vol. 2, ed. by Ronald W. Jones and Peter B. Kenen (Amsterdam: North-Holland).

Granger, C. W. J., 1981, "Some Properties of Time Series Data and Their Use in Econometric Model Specification," *Journal of Econometrics*, Vol. 16 (No. 1), pp. 121–30.

Group of Ten Deputies, 1993, *International Capital Movements and Foreign Exchange Markets: A Report to the Ministers and Governors* (Rome: Bank of Italy).

Harrod, R. F., 1939, *International Economics* (London: Nisbet and Co.).

International Monetary Fund, 2000, *World Economic Outlook, October 2000* (Washington).

Isard, Peter, 1995, *Exchange Rate Economics*, Cambridge Surveys of Economic Literature (Cambridge, England: Cambridge University Press).

———, and Steven Symansky, 1996, "Long-Run Movements in Real Exchange Rates," in *Exchange Rate Movements and Their Impact on Trade and Investment in the APEC Region*, IMF Occasional Paper No. 145, ed. by Takatoshi Ito, Peter Isard, Steven Symansky, and Tamim Bayoumi (Washington: International Monetary Fund).

Isard, Peter, and Hamid Faruqee, ed., 1998, *Exchange Rate Assessment: Extensions of the Macroeconomic Balance Approach*, IMF Occasional Paper No. 167 (Washington: International Monetary Fund).

Kahn, Robert, and Roger Nord, 1998, "Applications in IMF Surveillance Over Major Industrial Countries," in *Exchange Rate Assessment: Extensions of the Macroeconomic Balance Approach*, IMF Occasional Paper No. 167, ed. by Peter Isard and Hamid Faruqee (Washington: International Monetary Fund).

Knight, Malcolm D., and Paul R. Masson, 1988, "Fiscal Policies, Net Saving, and Real Exchange Rates: The United States, the Federal Republic of Germany, and Japan," in *International Aspects of Fiscal Policies*, ed. by Jacob Frenkel (Chicago: University of Chicago Press).

Krajnyák, Kornélia, 2000, "Switzerland's External Position in International Perspective," in IMF Staff Country Report No. 00/43 (Washington: International Monetary Fund).

Kravis, Irving B., Alan Heston, and Robert Summers, 1982, *World Product and Income: International Comparisons of Real Gross Product* (Baltimore: Johns Hopkins University Press).

Lane, Philip, and Gian Maria Milesi-Ferretti, 2001a, "Long-Term Capital Movements," IMF Working Paper No. 01/107 (Washington: International Monetary Fund); forthcoming in *NBER Macroeconomics Annual 2001.*

———, 2001b, "External Wealth, the Trade Balance, and the Real Exchange Rate" (unpublished).

———, 2001c, "The External Wealth of Nations: Measures of Foreign Assets and Liabilities for Industrial and Developing Countries," *Journal of International Economics*, Vol. 55 (December), pp. 263–94.

Laxton, Douglas, Peter Isard, Hamid Faruqee, Eswar Prasad, and Bart Turtelboom, 1998, *MULTIMOD Mark III: The Core Dynamic and Steady-State Models,* IMF Occasional Paper No. 164 (Washington: International Monetary Fund).

MacDonald, Ronald, 1999, "Exchange Rate Behaviour: Are Fundamentals Important?" *Economic Journal*, Vol. 109 (November), pp. F673–91.

Masson, Paul, 1998, "A Globally Consistent Conceptual Framework," in *Exchange Rate Assessment: Extensions of the Macroeconomic Balance Approach*, IMF Occasional Paper No. 167, ed. by Peter Isard and Hamid Faruqee (Washington: International Monetary Fund).

Meade, James E, 1951, *The Theory of International Economic Policy, Volume One: The Balance of Payments* (London: Oxford University Press).

Meese, Richard A. and Kenneth Rogoff, 1983a, "Empirical Exchange Rate Models of the Seventies: Do They Fit Out of Sample?" *Journal of International Economics*, Vol. 14 (February), pp. 3–24.

———, 1983b, "The Out-of-Sample Failure of Empirical Exchange Rate Models: Sampling Error or Misspecification?" in *Exchange Rates and International Macroeconomics*, ed. by Jacob A. Frenkel (Chicago: University of Chicago Press).

———, 1988, "Was It Real? The Exchange Rate–Interest Differential Relation Over the Modern Floating-Rate

Period," *Journal of Finance*, Vol. 43 (September), pp. 933–48.

Meredith, Guy, 1998, "A Dynamic Extension of the Macroeconomic Balance Approach," in *Exchange Rate Assessment: Extensions of the Macroeconomic Balance Approach*, IMF Occasional Paper No. 167, ed. by Peter Isard and Hamid Faruqee (Washington: International Monetary Fund).

Metzler, Lloyd A., 1951, "Wealth, Saving and the Rate of Interest," *Journal of Political Economy*, Vol. 59, pp. 930–46.

Moggridge, Daniel E., 1972, *British Monetary Policy, 1924–1931: The Norman Conquest of $4.86* (Cambridge, England: Cambridge University Press).

Mussa, Michael, 1984, "The Theory of Exchange Rate Determination," in *Exchange Rate Theory and Practice*, ed. by John F. O. Bilson and Richard C. Marston (Chicago: University of Chicago Press).

Nurkse, Ragnar, 1945, "Conditions of International Monetary Equilibrium," Essays in International Finance, No. 4 (Princeton, New Jersey: Princeton University Press).

Obstfeld, Maurice, and Kenneth Rogoff, 2000, "The Six Major Puzzles in International Macroeconomics: Is There a Common Cause?" in *NBER Macroeconomics Annual 2000*, ed. by B. Bernanke and K. Rogoff (Cambridge, Massachusetts: MIT Press).

Polak, Jacques J., 1995, "Fifty Years of Exchange Rate Research and Policy at the International Monetary Fund," *Staff Papers*, International Monetary Fund, Vol. 42 (December), pp. 734–61.

Ricardo, David,1821, "On the Principles of Political Economy and Taxation," reprinted in *The Works and Correspondence of David Ricardo*, Vol. I, ed. by Piero Sraffa (Cambridge, England: Cambridge University Press, 1951).

Rogoff, Kenneth, 1996, "The Purchasing Power Parity Puzzle," *Journal of Economic Literature*, Vol. 34 (June), pp. 647–68.

———, 1999, "Monetary Models of Dollar/Yen/Euro Nominal Exchange Rates: Dead or Undead?" *Economic Journal*, Vol. 109 (November), pp. F655–59.

Samuelson, Paul A., 1964, "Theoretical Notes on Trade Problems," *Review of Economics and Statistics*, Vol. 46 (May), pp. 145–54.

———, 1994, "Facets of Balassa-Samuelson Thirty Years Later," *Review of International Economics*, Vol. 2 (October), pp. 201–26.

Summers, Robert, and Alan Heston, 1991, "The Penn World Table (Mark 5): An Expanded Set of International Comparisons, 1950–1988," *Quarterly Journal of Economics*, Vol. 106 (May), pp. 327–68.

Swan, T. W., 1963, "Longer-Run Problems of the Balance of Payments," in *The Australian Economy: A Volume of Readings*, ed. by H. W. Arndt and W. M. Corden (Melbourne: F. W. Cheshire).

Williamson, John, 1985, *The Exchange Rate System* (Washington: Institute for International Economics).

———, ed., 1994, *Estimating Equilibrium Exchange Rates* (Washington: Institute for International Economics).

———, and Molly Mahar, 1998, "Current Account Targets," Appendix A in *Real Exchange Rates for the Year 2000*, ed. by Simon Wren-Lewis and Rebecca L. Driver (Washington: Institute for International Economics).

Recent Occasional Papers of the International Monetary Fund

209. Methodology for Current Account and Exchange Rate Assessments, by Peter Isard, Hamid Faruqee, G. Russell Kincaid, and Martin Fetherston. 2001.
208. Yemen in the 1990s: From Unification to Economic Reform, by Klaus Enders, Sherwyn Williams, Nada Choueiri, Yuri Sobolev, and Jan Walliser. 2001.
207. Malaysia: From Crisis to Recovery, by Kanitta Meesook, Il Houng Lee, Olin Liu, Yougesh Khatri, Natalia Tamirisa, Michael Moore, and Mark H. Krysl. 2001.
206. The Dominican Republic: Stabilization, Structural Reform, and Economic Growth, by Alessandro Giustiniani, Werner C. Keller, and Randa E. Sab. 2001.
205. Stabilization and Savings Funds for Nonrenewable Resources, by Jeffrey Davis, Rolando Ossowski, James Daniel, and Steven Barnett. 2001.
204. Monetary Union in West Africa (ECOWAS): Is It Desirable and How Could It Be Achieved? by Paul Masson and Catherine Pattillo. 2001.
203. Modern Banking and OTC Derivatives Markets: The Transformation of Global Finance and Its Implications for Systemic Risk, by Garry J. Schinasi, R. Sean Craig, Burkhard Drees, and Charles Kramer. 2000.
202. Adopting Inflation Targeting: Practical Issues for Emerging Market Countries, by Andrea Schaechter, Mark R. Stone, and Mark Zelmer. 2000.
201. Developments and Challenges in the Caribbean Region, by Samuel Itam, Simon Cueva, Erik Lundback, Janet Stotsky, and Stephen Tokarick. 2000.
200. Pension Reform in the Baltics: Issues and Prospects, by Jerald Schiff, Niko Hobdari, Axel Schimmelpfennig, and Roman Zytek. 2000.
199. Ghana: Economic Development in a Democratic Environment, by Sérgio Pereira Leite, Anthony Pellechio, Luisa Zanforlin, Girma Begashaw, Stefania Fabrizio, and Joachim Harnack. 2000.
198. Setting Up Treasuries in the Baltics, Russia, and Other Countries of the Former Soviet Union: An Assessment of IMF Technical Assistance, by Barry H. Potter and Jack Diamond. 2000.
197. Deposit Insurance: Actual and Good Practices, by Gillian G.H. Garcia. 2000.
196. Trade and Trade Policies in Eastern and Southern Africa, by a staff team led by Arvind Subramanian, with Enrique Gelbard, Richard Harmsen, Katrin Elborgh-Woytek, and Piroska Nagy. 2000.
195. The Eastern Caribbean Currency Union—Institutions, Performance, and Policy Issues, by Frits van Beek, José Roberto Rosales, Mayra Zermeño, Ruby Randall, and Jorge Shepherd. 2000.
194. Fiscal and Macroeconomic Impact of Privatization, by Jeffrey Davis, Rolando Ossowski, Thomas Richardson, and Steven Barnett. 2000.
193. Exchange Rate Regimes in an Increasingly Integrated World Economy, by Michael Mussa, Paul Masson, Alexander Swoboda, Esteban Jadresic, Paolo Mauro, and Andy Berg. 2000.
192. Macroprudential Indicators of Financial System Soundness, by a staff team led by Owen Evans, Alfredo M. Leone, Mahinder Gill, and Paul Hilbers. 2000.
191. Social Issues in IMF-Supported Programs, by Sanjeev Gupta, Louis Dicks-Mireaux, Ritha Khemani, Calvin McDonald, and Marijn Verhoeven. 2000.
190. Capital Controls: Country Experiences with Their Use and Liberalization, by Akira Ariyoshi, Karl Habermeier, Bernard Laurens, Inci Ötker-Robe, Jorge Iván Canales Kriljenko, and Andrei Kirilenko. 2000.
189. Current Account and External Sustainability in the Baltics, Russia, and Other Countries of the Former Soviet Union, by Donal McGettigan. 2000.
188. Financial Sector Crisis and Restructuring: Lessons from Asia, by Carl-Johan Lindgren, Tomás J.T. Baliño, Charles Enoch, Anne-Marie Gulde, Marc Quintyn, and Leslie Teo. 1999.
187. Philippines: Toward Sustainable and Rapid Growth, Recent Developments and the Agenda Ahead, by Markus Rodlauer, Prakash Loungani, Vivek Arora, Charalambos Christofides, Enrique G. De la Piedra, Piyabha Kongsamut, Kristina Kostial, Victoria Summers, and Athanasios Vamvakidis. 2000.
186. Anticipating Balance of Payments Crises: The Role of Early Warning Systems, by Andrew Berg, Eduardo Borensztein, Gian Maria Milesi-Ferretti, and Catherine Pattillo. 1999.

185. Oman Beyond the Oil Horizon: Policies Toward Sustainable Growth, edited by Ahsan Mansur and Volker Treichel. 1999.

184. Growth Experience in Transition Countries, 1990–98, by Oleh Havrylyshyn, Thomas Wolf, Julian Berengaut, Marta Castello-Branco, Ron van Rooden, and Valerie Mercer-Blackman. 1999.

183. Economic Reforms in Kazakhstan, Kyrgyz Republic, Tajikistan, Turkmenistan, and Uzbekistan, by Emine Gürgen, Harry Snoek, Jon Craig, Jimmy McHugh, Ivailo Izvorski, and Ron van Rooden. 1999.

182. Tax Reform in the Baltics, Russia, and Other Countries of the Former Soviet Union, by a staff team led by Liam Ebrill and Oleh Havrylyshyn. 1999.

181. The Netherlands: Transforming a Market Economy, by C. Maxwell Watson, Bas B. Bakker, Jan Kees Martijn, and Ioannis Halikias. 1999.

180. Revenue Implications of Trade Liberalization, by Liam Ebrill, Janet Stotsky, and Reint Gropp. 1999.

179. Disinflation in Transition: 1993–97, by Carlo Cottarelli and Peter Doyle. 1999.

178. IMF-Supported Programs in Indonesia, Korea, and Thailand: A Preliminary Assessment, by Timothy Lane, Atish Ghosh, Javier Hamann, Steven Phillips, Marianne Schulze-Ghattas, and Tsidi Tsikata. 1999.

177. Perspectives on Regional Unemployment in Europe, by Paolo Mauro, Eswar Prasad, and Antonio Spilimbergo. 1999.

176. Back to the Future: Postwar Reconstruction and Stabilization in Lebanon, edited by Sena Eken and Thomas Helbling. 1999.

175. Macroeconomic Developments in the Baltics, Russia, and Other Countries of the Former Soviet Union, 1992–97, by Luis M. Valdivieso. 1998.

174. Impact of EMU on Selected Non–European Union Countries, by R. Feldman, K. Nashashibi, R. Nord, P. Allum, D. Desruelle, K. Enders, R. Kahn, and H. Temprano-Arroyo. 1998.

173. The Baltic Countries: From Economic Stabilization to EU Accession, by Julian Berengaut, Augusto Lopez-Claros, Françoise Le Gall, Dennis Jones, Richard Stern, Ann-Margret Westin, Effie Psalida, Pietro Garibaldi. 1998.

172. Capital Account Liberalization: Theoretical and Practical Aspects, by a staff team led by Barry Eichengreen and Michael Mussa, with Giovanni Dell'Ariccia, Enrica Detragiache, Gian Maria Milesi-Ferretti, and Andrew Tweedie. 1998.

171. Monetary Policy in Dollarized Economies, by Tomás Baliño, Adam Bennett, and Eduardo Borensztein. 1998.

170. The West African Economic and Monetary Union: Recent Developments and Policy Issues, by a staff team led by Ernesto Hernández-Catá and comprising Christian A. François, Paul Masson, Pascal Bouvier, Patrick Peroz, Dominique Desruelle, and Athanasios Vamvakidis. 1998.

169. Financial Sector Development in Sub-Saharan African Countries, by Hassanali Mehran, Piero Ugolini, Jean Phillipe Briffaux, George Iden, Tonny Lybek, Stephen Swaray, and Peter Hayward. 1998.

168. Exit Strategies: Policy Options for Countries Seeking Greater Exchange Rate Flexibility, by a staff team led by Barry Eichengreen and Paul Masson with Hugh Bredenkamp, Barry Johnston, Javier Hamann, Esteban Jadresic, and Inci Ötker. 1998.

167. Exchange Rate Assessment: Extensions of the Macroeconomic Balance Approach, edited by Peter Isard and Hamid Faruqee. 1998

166. Hedge Funds and Financial Market Dynamics, by a staff team led by Barry Eichengreen and Donald Mathieson with Bankim Chadha, Anne Jansen, Laura Kodres, and Sunil Sharma. 1998.

165. Algeria: Stabilization and Transition to the Market, by Karim Nashashibi, Patricia Alonso-Gamo, Stefania Bazzoni, Alain Féler, Nicole Laframboise, and Sebastian Paris Horvitz. 1998.

164. MULTIMOD Mark III: The Core Dynamic and Steady-State Model, by Douglas Laxton, Peter Isard, Hamid Faruqee, Eswar Prasad, and Bart Turtelboom. 1998.

163. Egypt: Beyond Stabilization, Toward a Dynamic Market Economy, by a staff team led by Howard Handy. 1998.

Note: For information on the title and availability of Occasional Papers not listed, please consult the IMF Publications Catalog or contact IMF Publication Services.